DEAR AUTHOR...

DEAR AUTHOR...

Michael Legat

Allison & Busby
Published by W.H. Allen & Co. Plc

An Allison & Busby book
Published by
W.H. Allen & Co. Plc
Sekforde House
175/9 St John Street
London EC1V 4LL

First published 1972, reprinted 1973

This revised edition first published by
Allison & Busby 1989

Printed in Great Britain by
Cox & Wyman Ltd, Reading, Berkshire

ISBN 0 85031 923 4

INTRODUCTION

Dear Author... was originally published in 1972, at which time I was Editorial Director of Corgi Books. It has now been updated and revised, but it remains a work written from the standpoint of a paperback publisher concerned primarily with fiction, though I believe, as with the original edition, that its interest and application will extend beyond that somewhat limited field.

One of the biggest problems in the publishing world is that very few authors understand much about the trade. This book attempts to explain some of the matters which frequently cause trouble. There are letters for the beginner (who can so easily put a foot wrong, and for whom a little know-how might work wonders) and for the old hand (who often knows a little less than he or she thinks). As well as writing about general publishing matters and procedures I have included a few specifically editorial letters, and I hope that these, though ostensibly concerned with individual books (and those exclusively novels) will be of help to writers in all genres.

Above all it is my wish to convince authors of two things: that their problems are not unique, and that the failings of publishers are more often due to human inadequacy than to a deliberate malice towards their authors. I have tried to be fair to both sides, but if at times I sound like a P.R.O. for the publishing industry, I apologise. Perhaps I do so because such an animal is so badly needed.

I need hardly say that the letters (and their correspondents) are imaginary – but the problems they deal with are all ones that I met on many occasions during my thirty-five years as a publisher. There is perhaps equally no need to point out that a book of this kind must contain a certain number of generalisations, but I should make it clear that the opinions expressed are mine alone and it must not be assumed that they are necessarily those of my present publishers, or of those companies for whom I worked, or, indeed, of the entire publishing trade.

Finally, I should like to thank all the authors with whom I worked over so many years, and whose questions and difficulties provided the basic material for the book. I also want to acknowledge with gratitude my immense debts to Brian Cleeve, who put the idea of the book into my mind, to Diane Pearson, for her encouragement and extremely helpful comments, and to my publisher for giving me the chance to produce this revised edition.

M.L.

1

To a member of the public who asks for advice on how to become an author

Dear Sir,

Thank you for your letter.

There is a standard reply to your enquiry. It says that you should practise writing, and you should read as much as possible so that you may learn how other writers do their job. Sometimes additional suggestions are made, such as getting a critical friend to tell you what he thinks of your writing, or making a habit of writing to your local newspaper on a variety of subjects in order to extend your range of vocabulary and to teach you to express yourself clearly and succinctly.

I don't think that any publishers normally advise beginners to join a correspondence course in writing, though I do know of one very successful author who started that way, so perhaps it is worth considering.

All publishers will advise you to read a lot—partly because it's good advice, and partly because it's good for business.

But there are other things which need saying.

First of all I should like to ask why you want to become an author.

If your sole reason for wanting to write is to make money, then I should advise you to give up here and now. Being an author is not a get-rich-quick occupation. More often than not the money that is earned from writing is minute in comparison with the labour put into the job. Of course there are some authors who have achieved fame and fortune overnight; they have been either exceptionally talented or exceptionally lucky (or both).

Equally if you feel that it is an easy thing to do, whether or not the money it brings in is substantial, and that therefore you might as well try your hand, I should advise you to think again. Writing is hard work, very hard work, and often very lonely work, and again it is only the extraordinarily gifted or fortunate authors who can produce a book without slaving at it, sometimes even hating it, and keeping their noses tight up against the grindstone. The really professional author often ties himself to a working day that most other people would consider to be intolerably long.

On the other hand, if you have a compulsion to write—and I mean a compulsion, not an occasional vague urge—if you are absolutely determined to get into print, if you are prepared for an extremely hard working life and possibly very little reward, then maybe you have a chance of becoming an author. And if you always had good marks at school for English composition and have some understanding of the mysteries of commas and semi-colons, and if when you tell a joke or the story of your holidays you have the knack of keeping your friends interested and amused, then your chance may be a better one.

You probably don't need advice anyway, because the driving force inside you will teach you what you want to know. But if at this stage you insist on some words of counsel, then go back to that standard reply: practise your writing, and read and read and read. And good luck.

Yours truly,

2

Dear Sir,

Thank you for your enquiry about the publication of a book. The first step, of course, is to submit your book to a publisher. For this purpose it should be typed in double spacing on one side of the paper only. Most publishers make this a condition, and will not consider a hand-written book. Regular typing paper is preferable to smaller sizes of paper, and lined paper should be avoided.

Do make sure that at least one carbon copy of the book is made at the time it is typed, so that if anything happens to the top copy you still have a typescript from which to work.

When you send your typescript to the publisher you should enclose stamps or a postal order to cover the return of the book if it should prove unsuitable for the publisher. Make certain that your name and address is on the typescript—preferably on both front and back pages.

Not all publishers are interested in all kinds of books—some specialise and publish only plays, or religous works, or educational books—and it is well to choose with some care which publisher or publishers you will submit your book to. Probably the best way of doing this is to look for a publisher who has recently brought out books in the same style as your own. There are always exceptions, and publishers who normally never publish a sports book, for instance, might do so if the right one were offered to them at the right moment. But by and large it is less time-wasting to select a publisher who is more likely to be interested because he already publishes your kind of book.

Once you have picked out a publisher it is courteous, and frequently saves time, money and effort, to write to him and ask whether you may submit your book for his consideration. If he refuses, don't be angry or depressed; his reasons for turning you down may be valid for him, but may not be shared by the next publisher you try.

If the publisher agrees to read your work, post it or deliver it to his offices. You may expect to receive a prompt acknowledgement of its safe arrival, but the verdict may take quite a while to reach you—don't be surprised if it takes six weeks or more.

You can save yourself a great deal of the trouble involved in selecting a publisher and making sure that he is willing to read your book by sending it initially to a literary agent, whose job it is to perform all these functions on your behalf. However, it has to be said that it is often more difficult to find an agent who is willing to handle your work than to place it with a publisher by direct submission.

You will find the addresses of both publishers and agents in such books as *The Writers' and Artists' Yearbook*, *The Writer's Handbook* and *The Book Writer's Handbook*, which should be available in your public library.

Yours truly,

3

To an author who asks whether to submit all of his book or simply a synopsis and specimen chapter

Dear Sir,

Thank you for your letter.

If your book has been completed, then it is much better that you should send the whole thing. It is certainly easier to make a judgment that way.

The only value in sending synopses and specimen chapters is for the author who hasn't completed his book and doesn't want to do so unless he gets positive encouragement on the basis of the work he has done so far. In asking for this he naturally takes a risk, because, even to a publisher's practised eye, a synopsis and specimen chapter (or chapters) do not always reveal a book's merits (or demerits!).

It is possible, however, to obtain a commission to write certain non-fiction books on the basis of a detailed synopsis and specimen chapters, but is less likely to occur with fiction, unless the publisher already knows your work.

Yours truly,

4

Dear Sir,

Thank you for your letter.

The answer to your query is that it shouldn't cost you anything to have a book published. Normally, publishers pay you for the privilege of publishing your book. They may not pay you very large sums, but they do pay you—not the other way round.

Your costs should be limited to the typing of the manuscript, the paper it is typed on, and postage. You may also be involved in expenses while writing the book: travel, research, postage again. Incidentally, all your expenses should be recorded because you can claim tax relief on them against earnings from your book. But the cost of setting the book in type, printing it, binding it, publicising it, distributing it—all these are the publisher's responsibility.

Vanity publishing is only for rich authors. It costs a lot of money and you are unlikely to get any of it back, despite the fulsome promises the vanity publisher will make.

Regular publishers can occasionally be persuaded to take on books which are subsidised in some way, perhaps by a commercial concern which sees the books as useful publicity, or simply by a wealthy author contributing to the costs. But no reputable publisher would take on such work unless it had some genuine literary merit, whereas vanity publishers accept any old rubbish.

Tell me more about your book. If what you say interests us, I'll ask you to send it to us so that we can read it. If we then decide to publish, I'll write and let you know how much *we* would be prepared to pay *you*!

Yours truly,

5

To an author who asks how long I require a book to be

Dear Madam,

Thank you for your letter.

Your question is not an entirely easy one to answer. Let me start by stating a principle, and then follow up with some qualifications of it.

The principle is this: a book should be as long as it wants to be—not as long as the publisher wants it to be, nor even necessarily as long as the author may think he or she wants it to be, but just as many words as are needed to tell the story or cover the subject. Fewer words than this, and the book will be cramped; more words, and it will be padded.

Now for the qualifications. Publishers bring out some of their books in series, and for these a specific length may be essential, in order to maintain uniformity. Publishers are also affected by economics and may well say: 'for a book of this kind I cannot charge more than such-and-such a price, therefore I do not want the book to be more than so many thousand words'. Economics sometimes affects very long books too, and because they are so expensive to produce, publishers may flinch away from them completely (unless they are by established authors with huge followings, which means that an unusually large first printing is possible, and that for this reason the price can be kept down). Very short books pose a problem too, because they are not much cheaper to produce than a standard length book, and must therefore be priced in a way that looks expensive—as though value for money is not being given—and this in turn may hamper sales.

I would suggest that for beginners it will be very difficult to sell a book to a publisher if it is less than 35,000 words or more than 120,000 words. Something between 50,000 and 75,000 words is more likely to get you a contract. But there are always exceptions—quality can break all the rules—and let me remind you again that if your book *demands* to be outside these limits you should not argue, for the book is probably right. Try to make sure that it is.

By the way, when you have finished your book you don't have to count every single word so that you can present it to the publisher with the information that the typescript contains, say, 53,287 words. Assuming your typing is reasonably even, discover the average number of words in a line (by counting the words in several lines and dividing the total words by the number of lines you have counted), multiply this figure by the number of lines to a normal full page, and multiply that figure by the number of pages in your typescript. Don't worry about the fact that the pages at the end of chapters may not have the full number of lines on them, unless there is a particularly large number of such pages. Round your total words figure off to the nearest thousand, and put on the title page: 'Approximately 53,000 words' (or whatever figure you've reached).

Actually, you don't really need to go to all this trouble anyway, because publishers are fairly expert at gauging the length of a typescript just by a quick glance, and they can always verify their guess quite easily by getting someone from their production department to do what is called a 'cast-off' (a word count).

I hope this letter gives you the information you need.

Yours truly,

6

To an author who asks if we ever commission books

Dear Sir,

Thank you for your letter.

We do indeed commission books, and so do most publishers, but only under certain circumstances. It really boils down to the author having something special to offer—perhaps his life story, if he is a famous person or has had a particularly fascinating career, or perhaps his expert knowledge of some particular subject (for instance, one might commission a book on photography, and would obviously choose an author who was expert at it). In the case of fiction, commissions do occur, but again the author must have something unusual to offer—perhaps it is to be a novel with a specialist background, or the author himself has considerable fame in another sphere, or the publisher has what he thinks is a splendid idea for a plot and needs someone to write it for him.

But in all these cases one extra ingredient is needed, and that is some proof that the author in question can write. Most commissions, in my experience, are given to already practised writers. At the very least, from an inexperienced author a publisher would require a lengthy synopsis, some specimen chapters and probably several hours of meetings and discussions.

The publisher will also want to know why a commission is necessary, since most authors are content to starve in garrets while they write their masterpieces, which they only then try to sell. Why is the publisher being asked to pay in advance for this particular book? Because the author won't write it unless he is guaranteed publication? Because he needs some finance in advance in order to research the book? Or because he needs to devote all his time to the book and must have something to live on while he is writing it? These or other reasons will be considered by the publisher and found acceptable or not according to circumstances.

In any case, however, publishers are finding it more and more difficult to commission books because of a shortage of available funds. The point is that most publishers do not have spare cash—their money is always tied up in future projects, their profit is always ploughed back into their forthcoming books, and of course, since publishing is a very chancy business, a vast amount of their capital is invested in books which are lying in their warehouses, waiting with varying degrees of expectation to be sold. The result of all this is that publishers tend to live off overdrafts, and the interest on overdrawn bank accounts is very high these days. In other words, money is expensive, and publishers can't afford to commission as freely as they used to.

I trust this letter gives you the information you were seeking.

Yours truly,

7

To an author who asks how much he is likely to earn from the publication of a book

Dear Sir,

Thank you for your letter. The question of how much you can earn from a book is like asking how long is a piece of string; but I will try to give you some general pointers.

Single books earn anything from nothing to millions of pounds. Assuming that your book is accepted for publication, you will probably receive not less than £100 and not more than £1000 as an advance (I am also assuming that you are an unknown writer and that this is your first acceptance). This sum will be set against royalties on the publisher's edition or editions of your book, and also against any other sums of money which come to him from the book.

Let us leave those extra sums for the moment and concentrate on the royalties. The normal practise is for the publisher to pay you a percentage of the retail price of the book on every copy of it that he sells. Since you have been given an advance, you will not receive any more money from royalties until sufficient copies have been sold to earn the advance.

Suppose you have received an advance of £1000, the royalty is 10% and the retail price of the book is £9.95. You will be earning a royalty of 99.5p per copy sold, but you will not receive any money above the advance paid until more than 1,000 copies have been sold. (It doesn't work out quite as simply as this in practice, since royalty rates vary according to the price at which the publisher sells the books, but the basic principle of setting earnings against the advance is still valid.)

But in fact royalties are not the only source of income. If you are lucky the publisher may sell paperback rights, or translation rights, or serial rights, or a number of other different subsidiary rights. Any monies he receives from such sales will, after he has taken his percentage according to the arrangements in the contract, be set against that original advance.

Those are, in the briefest of outlines, the mechanics of the matter.

Now, how do they work in practice? A recent survey carried out by the Society of Authors showed that the average yearly earnings of authors were quite appallingly low.

I would say that the unestablished author who makes £1,500 out of his first book is not doing at all badly. If you can rake in £10,000 you can count yourself as successful, and once you're over that level you're getting to be big business. (All this just goes to show that there are easier ways of earning a living than by being an author. And this is why more and more authors have to do their writing in their spare time nowadays, while earning their living from some less unpredictable form of employment. The number of writers who can exist solely on the income from their writings is declining year by year, and even many established authors find that they have to supplement their earnings with lecture tours or television appearances or other personality-cult activities.)

Of course, if you are really lucky you may become eventually one of the top-selling authors with an income in the six or even seven figure range. Once in the bluest of moons this happens with a first book. Don't count on it happening to you, or get discouraged if it doesn't. The book business is no fairer than life itself, and though most of the big-name authors fully deserve their success, the actual size of the success is sometimes out of proportion to the size of their talent. It is like the pop stars who earn such fabulous sums: many of them are very gifted and the reward is fair; others receive money and acclamation on a scale far beyond that which they deserve; and there are others who, talented or not, find that recognition eludes them. It's the same with books.

Yours truly,

8

Dear Sir,

Thank you for your letter enquiring about the processes of publishing. There is a very simple answer—get hold of a copy of *The Truth About Publishing* by Sir Stanley Unwin. It is comprehensive and readily understandable and was written by one of the greatest publishers the world has ever known. The book is published by Unwin Hyman Ltd.

Yours truly,

9

My dear Andrea,

I was enchanted to have such a charming and totally undeserved letter from you. I am still blushing over some of the flattering things you say. Thank you. Thank you. Thank you.

I must take issue with you on one point, however. I was astonished to see that you think me 'so sane'. My dear Andrea, I beg to inform you that I am as neurotic as they come and mad whether the wind is north-north-west or not—and everyone I know in publishing is in the same boat.

After all, we have good reason. Publishing is really the most ridiculous business one could imagine. Our auditors, sober, industrious, and I have no doubt sane to a man, just cannot understand why we should bother with so uncertain a method of earning a living. They smile when they talk to us, as though we were irresponsible children—and of course they're right. What other well-conducted business could consider producing in the next twelve months nearly three hundred products, each different from the other, at different prices, produced in different quantities, aimed at different sections of a market about which we know very little anyway, and which vary in cost to us by extraordinarily large amounts not often reflected in the retail price? And moreover we have no certainty of selling any of those products in the quantities we have produced.

Edward Garnett once wrote to Lawrence of Arabia about the publisher Jonathan Cape: 'Like all publishers, he lives on great expectations of the most nebulous order.'

Some time ago someone asked me if I gambled. I replied that I did not, because I don't do the pools and I don't count the raffle tickets at the church bazaar or the occasional ten pence which etiquette compels me to flutter in the office Derby draw and which is the sum total of my interest in horse, dog or any other kind of racing on which people bet. And then, thinking about it afterwards, I realised why I have no need of roulette or bookies or homes, aways and draws—I gamble every day of my working life. My whole business, and that of every general publisher, is a gamble. No wonder we're all dotty!

But there is worse to come. Can you believe that anyone could remain sane in a business which is not only subject to all the follies I've already mentioned, a business incidentally which also makes incredible demands on one's so-called 'free' time, but one which depends in the first place for its products on an even more unstable group of people? I am referring of course to authors. 'Publishing,' said (I believe) Sir Frederick Macmillan, 'would be fun if it weren't for authors.' His tongue, it goes without saying, was in his cheek, but he was right. Absolutely right. On the whole authors are lovable but impossible. Fickle, temperamental, unreliable, vain, greedy monsters —that's what authors are. But I love 'em and would hate not to work with 'em. Isn't that proof of my madness?

Of course there are a few sweet and marvellous exceptions like yourself, my dear Andrea, without whom I and my fellow publishers would undoubtedly find ourselves locked up in a booby hatch. Even there I imagine we would start persuading the other inmates to start scribbling their masterpieces and then to submit them for our consideration!

My thanks again and my love.

Madly,

10

Dear Sir,

I am sorry but I must decline your kind offer to show me your collection of short stories. No publisher, to my knowledge, seems able to find a good market for books in this category. I think this is a shame and also something of a mystery, since nearly everyone I speak to on the subject admits to liking short stories. Presumably none of these people is a book buyer, because volumes of short stories certainly don't sell.

There are a few exceptions to this rule. Those by very eminent authors sell, though in lesser quantities usually than their full-length books. And science fiction and horror stories find a market. Otherwise the prospects are bleak and publishers who are bold enough or foolish enough to try to crack the problem are sometimes driven to attempts to disguise from the public exactly what the books are. It rarely works.

I am sorry not to be more encouraging.

Yours truly,

11

Dear Sir,

Thank you for your letter asking if we would be interested in a book on the present crisis at Barchester University.

I have to say that I am most doubtful about this kind of project which depends so much for its saleability on its topical nature. In the United States publishers have been very successful with what they call 'instant' books—topical books which they have published at the time of the event in question or perhaps as little as three days after it. There are however two factors in the British industry which make it very difficult to emulate our friends in American publishing houses.

Firstly, although our printers can work at great speed, they seem to find it difficult to perform the miracles that American printers have achieved. And it isn't only the printers who have to produce the book in an unbelievably short time. The author has to write his book at breakneck speed, and the publisher has to rush all his processes too. The only way to achieve all this exceptionally fast work is by paying for it. Most of it means overtime, and that costs the earth. So we have the problem of getting people to work very much faster than usual, and on top of that we have the question of whether the book is going to be economic anyway (a matter which tends to be less in doubt for the American publisher since his market is a bigger one than ours, which gives a better chance of absorbing the extra costs).

The second point is perhaps even more relevant. I do not believe that the British public is as interested in this kind of topical book as the American public, partly because we tend to concentrate on football rather than burning social questions, but even more because of the good reason that in this country we have a national press of high quality. Because it is national rather than local, it gives particularly thorough coverage to a news story of this type, and since we are a nation of newspaper readers, we all read 'all about it'. We are perhaps not so anxious to read it again in book form.

I think there is also a fallacy in the argument that, for instance, 'there are hundreds and thousands of students and teachers in the country, let alone all the parents and other indirectly involved people, and they'll all want to read this book'. Well, I'm afraid they won't. A few perhaps, but the majority will be made up of those who either know it all or don't care anyway.

I'm sorry, then, to have to turn down your offer. Thank you nonetheless for the opportunity of considering it.

Yours truly,

12

To an author who asks if I will consider her books, which she describes, and who asks additionally what my requirements are

Dear Madam,

Thank you for your letter. I do in fact almost always have room for books of the kind you describe, and I must say it is a pleasure to find someone taking the trouble to ask what sort of books I want.

First of all, I am looking, as is every publisher, for that splendid unique book which combines literary merit with commercial possibilities of a high order, which is extraordinary and original, and which will make its author's reputation and certainly enhance its publisher's.

Apart from that little pipe dream, what I really want is three A's.

First, A for Action. I don't necessarily mean physical action, but I do want something to happen in the book, and indeed I prefer to have quite a lot of things happening. I want a body on page one, if I may speak metaphorically—by which I mean that, whatever kind of book it is, I want something interesting to happen at a very early stage. Then I want the interest to carry on with as little flagging as possible to the end, and then to stop. I must admit, you see, to being old-fashioned enough to like my books to have a beginning, a middle and an end.

Secondly, A for Authenticity. I mean by this that I want to be able to believe in the book, and especially in its background. This seems to me to be an age which demands greater expertise from its creative people than past periods have done. For instance, it is no longer enough for a writer to say that a character is an American, to call him 'Hank' and to sprinkle his speeches with 'say' and 'I guess' and other such locutions; nowadays, the author must create an American character with authentic speech patterns and behaviour and a genuine background. Nor can we accept, as another example, a story about an ordinary present-day middle-class family if it endows them with servants—nobody has a maid nowadays. Television has brought the reality of the world into every home, and many of the most successful fictional television programmes owe much of their success to the documentary nature of their backgrounds. This trend has been reflected in novels too, and in every category of fiction (even in fantasy) the current demand is for believable stories set against well-documented backgrounds. Authenticity is also required in matters like the behaviour of characters and the lack of wild coincidences or dei ex machina.

Thirdly, A for Authorship. By this I mean not only that the author should be able to write reasonably good English, and preferably have some slight knowledge of syntax, paragraphing, punctuation and spelling, but also that he should have an idea of how to tell a story; of how to keep suspense going; of when to break from one set of characters in order to introduce a subplot; of how to end a book without leaving loose ends untied; of how to give the reader enough information, but not too much; of how to maintain a balance between descriptive passages, action and speech; and so on and so on. I once heard someone giving a talk on this sort of thing and laying down all kinds of rigid rules about it. Well, I don't think you can make rules about it—you have to learn it by experience and by looking at the work of those who have Authorship in high degree.

I hope that all this helps, and if you feel that your books will meet at least some of my demands, by all means send them to me.

Yours truly,

13

Dear Sir,

Thank you for your letter offering to show us your novel entitled *Norwegian Treasure*.

I would be very willing to consider the book, and if you will deliver it to our offices, as you suggest, I will try to let you have a quick decision.

I must however ask you to forgive me if I do not take you up on your offer to talk to me about the book when you deliver it. May I be blunt, sir? I am a rather busy man. I do not really have time to spare on someone who may or may not be of interest to me (if your *book* is of interest to me than I will spare you all the time I can—but that comes later). And what is there about the book that you cannot explain to me in a letter? And shouldn't the book speak for itself anyway? After all, you won't be able to go round to all the people who buy it in order to explain it to them.

No, sir, if you want to tell me something unusual about the typescript—that it has a special appeal to septuagenarian widowers living in Liverpool, or that this is a first draft and you are willing to alter it in any way I want, or that you are not really homosexual despite the content of the book, or that the Mafia will get me if I don't publish it (or alternatively that God has revealed to you not only that He wishes you to write a book but also that He wishes me to publish it), or that your firm is willing to underwrite its publication to the magnificent extent of purchasing twenty-five copies at best trade terms—dear, sir, please put this vital information into writing or let the wretched book have the chance of conveying it to me all by itself.

Yours truly,

14

Dear Sir,

Thank you for your letter offering to show me your book which I will willingly consider if you will send it to me.

I should like to point out however that the fact that so many of your friends like it is no guarantee that I will. I do not know your friends and therefore have no idea whether they are good judges or bad, but even if I were told that they were real experts I should still prefer to make up my own mind unaided.

I must admit on the other hand that if any of your friends also happen to be friends of mine, then I should be interested to hear their opinions. This is not because I would necessarily be influenced by my friends—but I should be able to assess their comments in the light of my knowledge of the people making them, and then what they had to say might have a value for me.

But in general the rule is to let the book speak for itself. A good book is its own best salesman at every stage of its career.

Yours truly,

15

To an author who asks, in view of the recent news that the Bishop of Barchester is to marry his housekeeper, if I will consider publishing a paperback edition of his now out-of-print novel, since it deals with the self same theme

Dear Mr. Jones,

Of course I remember you. I am always pleased when the authors I have met when addressing Writers' Circles do in fact get in touch with me again, so I was particularly pleased to have your letter.

I would certainly be willing to consider your book, Mr. Jones, just as I will consider any book which might be suitable for my list, but I shall not be looking at it with any thoughts of tying-in with the news about the Bishop.

Novels *can* be sold because they have a connection with some topical news item, but I'm afraid it has to be something rather more world-shaking than a Bishop marrying his housekeeper. It has to be an event of considerable importance and, especially, of lasting interest. You see, the announcement about the Bishop will not be followed by another item in tomorrow's paper—it isn't even a nine days' wonder, it's here today and gone tomorrow. And even if it caught the public imagination, would it last as a news item for the nine months or so that it would take to get your book on to the market? I'm afraid it would have been long forgotten.

I hope you understand my point. If you would still like to send me your book, please do so.

With best wishes.

Yours sincerely,

16

To an author who begs me to explain why I have turned down his offer to write for me

Dear Mr. Hackbridge,

Like most publishers, I prefer not to enter into this sort of correspondence, but I hope you will forgive me (yes, I mean that, for I don't think you will enjoy this letter) if I do so in this case.

Let me recap. You wrote to me saying that you are an author with some fifty published books to your credit, that you have worked for a large number of publishers, that you are professional in your approach and realistic in your expectation of monetary reward. So far so good. And then you offer to write for me any kind of book I want, of any length, on any subject, and you promise a swift delivery.

Well, Mr. Hackbridge, that was where you lost me. You see, I am quite sure that you would have written me a 'publishable' western, crime story, biography, sex epic or whatever, but I'm afraid that I don't want something that is merely 'publishable'. I don't want anything that is written not because you have any desire to write it, but simply to supply a supposed need of mine. I don't want a book that is simply competent, and basically dull and uninspiring, and probably very much the same as all your fifty other books.

It is possible of course that you are very much better than the average 'I-can-write-anything' author, and you might argue that a really competent professional *can* write anything at all, to order. If you are as good as that, I am doing you an injustice, and I apologise.

I think, however, Mr. Hackbridge, that you are probably no better and no worse than most of your kind, and I'm afraid that before too many years have passed you are going to find it difficult to make a living from writing this sort of book. Gradually, as the commercial world impinges more and more on what used to be an occupation for gentlemen, it is getting tougher for publishers and authors to get away with mediocrity.

I am sorry. I have just remembered one way in which I may be able to use your talents in the future (if, after reading this letter, you would still be willing to work for me). I do occasionally want what is called a novelisation of a screenplay, or in other words a novel based on the script for a film. A horrible thought, I agree, but if I may advise you, Mr. Hackbridge, I would suggest you make a speciality of that kind of writing. I certainly can't see any other good prospects for you.

Forgive my frankness.

Yours sincerely,

17

Dear Sir,

Thank you for your letter regarding the typescript that you sent to us last week.

We will try to give you a decision about it as soon as possible, but it may be a further fortnight or so before we can do so.

In case you feel that we are keeping you waiting for a very long time—after all, it only takes a few hours to read a book—let me explain that there is never an occasion when I and my colleagues in the editorial department are without a pile of books to read. Sometimes the piles are bigger than at other times, and that means that it then takes longer to deal with new submissions.

The new books go to the bottom of the piles and work their way up. It isn't always a steady progression to the top of the pile—sometimes a book will arrive that has to be read very quickly (it might be, for instance, a book by a major and extremely successful author—and once an author is in that position he and his agent and his hardcover publisher are able to demand very speedy decisions), or perhaps a book has been in our hands for some time already and has been read by one of my colleagues who now wants me to read it before a final decision is made (some books get four or five readings before we make up our minds to accept or reject), and it too would get priority.

We have something like one thousand books a year submitted to us. We do our best to look at them quickly, but some delay is inevitable. Since practically every publisher is unbearably slow from the author's point of view, whether his book is being considered or put into production or sold, I can only ask on my own behalf and that of my publishing colleagues for your patience and that of your fellow authors. Believe me, we will let you have the verdict at the earliest possible moment.

Yours truly,

18

Dear Sir,

Thank you for your letter concerning your typescript *Death in Welwyn Garden City* which we returned to you recently.

I must be honest and say that I am not surprised to learn that the hair which you placed between pages 172 and 173 of the typescript is still there. But it really does not mean, as you believe, that your book was not seriously considered.

Let me explain. Very few books submitted to a publisher are sent back without being looked at. Those that are rejected without even being opened are usually books totally unsuited to the list of the publisher in question. For instance, I am a publisher of popular entertainment fiction in paperback form. If someone sends me a biography of an obscure sixteenth-century Bulgarian poet, or a treatise on transistorised diesel engines, or the life of the lesser green woodpecker, I am likely to send the typescripts back unread by return of post because, even if the Bulgarian poet had an extraordinarily varied sex life, even if transistorised diesels are going to transform rail transport, even if a film about the lesser green woodpecker is going to be shown on BBC 2 next Sunday, these are books which just do not fit into our line. However good they are we couldn't begin to sell them.

Your book of course is not in this category. It is a thriller and I do publish thrillers. So it was looked at—not necessarily read all the way through, but looked at.

If one works as a publisher's editor or reader, one acquires certain skills. One of these is to judge very quickly whether a typescript is *not* of interest to the publishing firm for which one works. Do please note what I said then: on behalf of one's own firm one can decide quickly against a book. Deciding in favour of a book is usually a more lengthy business. Making a judgment about its prospects of publication by some other firm is not the reader's job.

So what happens? The reader picks up the typescript and reads the first few pages. As a result he may know straight away that his firm will not want to publish the book, perhaps because the book is very badly written, perhaps because those few pages have revealed that it is a type of book in which the publisher is not interested.

Sometimes of course the first pages are interesting enough for the reader to want to see more of the book before making up his mind. He may read on, or he may turn the pages of the typescript over and read a passage from the middle of the book. I can hear your anguish as I dictate these words. 'That book cost me sweat and blood,' you shriek, 'and I didn't write it for it to get that sort of treatment!' But do remember that the people who are giving it this treatment are professionals who know what they are looking for and how to look for it. This kind of sampling can be very revealing to the experienced eye.

Another method that the reader may use is 'skip-reading'. This means of course that he does not read every word of the book—he skips a paragraph here, a paragraph there, perhaps a page or a few pages, but he does read enough to discover what kind of book he is dealing with, and when he has finished he can probably tell you the plot in considerable detail despite the fact that he didn't read every word. It's a technique, a trick of the trade, and anyone with the basic aptitude can learn to do it.

A further development of this method is what I call 'skim-reading', in which a really experienced editor can leaf through a book or typescript in a few minutes, letting his eyes drift over the pages as he turns them, and still have, when he has turned the last page, a more than merely rough idea of the contents.

Of course, the better the book and the more suited to the publisher's list it is, the more time and trouble the editor will take with it. Over the years I have found that an inability to skip-read any particular book is a very reliable indication that it is of outstanding quality.

Well, sir, I have not been through our records to find out at what stage your book was rejected, but I am sure that it received serious consideration. We may have made a mistake—naturally we do from time to time—but if so, it is an error of judgment rather than a question of not having bothered. After all, no publisher can afford simply to make a casual decision to send a typescript back unread providing it appears to be at all possible for him and his list—he might be turning down the best-seller of the century.

One last point: do please remember that the verdict against your book has been made on behalf of my firm only. Another publisher may feel very differently about your work, and I hope that you do in fact find enthusiasm elsewhere.

Yours truly,

P.S. About that hair between pages 172 and 173—publishers have been known to notice this sort of booby-trap and to make sure that the hair is carefully replaced when the typescript is returned!

19

Dear Mr. Robinson,

Thank you for your letter about your typescript which we returned to you recently.

You are quite right in supposing that I cannot enter into correspondence about the reason for the rejection of a book. Why? Well, imagine, Mr. Robinson, how much time I would spend, on books which I should not be publishing, if I were to agree to discuss all our negative decisions. We must turn down at least a dozen books a week. I should forever be writing letters and never getting on with the business of working on the books that I *am* going to publish.

Then how can an author learn if no one will give him any criticism? A valid question, and I don't have a very good answer to it. The trouble is that it is not my job or that of any other publisher to act as an instructor in the art of writing publishable books—there are more than enough of them around anyway, so we are in a buyers' market—and even if you and other authors were to offer to pay us for our advice, we do not have the time to help, because our own work keeps us too busy.

I can only suggest that you should make use of your friends, especially those who are habitual readers. Get them to read your book and persaude them to give you an honest criticism. Try asking your former English teacher—he or she would probably be flattered to be asked and would willingly give you an opinion.

If all your friends honestly assure you that the book is good, if you are confident that you know the technical job of writing and are not ignoring the rules of grammar, and if you are certain that you are submitting the book to the right kind of publisher (one who regularly publishes books of the same type as your own), then I can only suggest that you go on trying. I know one very successful author whose first novel was rejected nineteen times by different publishers,

and then the twentieth on the list accepted it with great enthusiasm.
Good luck!

Yours truly,

20

Dear Mr. Worthington,

This is a letter I shall not put in the post. Instead, I shall send you a polite, uninformative rejection slip, of if I do write a letter it will not say very much more than the rejection slip would—perhaps just that you could send your book to another publisher since our own negative verdict might easily be a wrong one.

What I should like to do is to write and say: please, Mr. Worthington, dear Mr. Worthington, why don't you just give up? You will never get a book published in a million years, because you have no talent. You can't spell, you can't punctuate, you have no feeling at all for words, your characters are lifeless, you have no narrative ability, you are not even observant enough to notice that books normally consist of something more than approximately seven thousand words (which is the length of your novel, which, incidentally, you have divided into twenty-eight chapters!). Add to all these faults the fact that your plot, sketchy though it is, is a direct pinch from a part of one of Mr. Ian Fleming's James Bond stories, and you can't even claim imagination and originality.

The trouble is, of course, that someone once said that everyone has a book in him. Whoever said it should have been strangled at birth. Ever since that saying became current, every idiot who wants to become as wealthy as Jeffrey Archer believes that all he has to do is to sit down and write the book that happens to be in him. He doesn't believe that writing is a craft which has to be learnt, often painfully and over a long period of time.

Of course, I would not deny the essential truth of that little saying in the sense that most people's lives can provide material for a book. But the gift of turning that inner material into readable, interesting words, sentences, paragraphs, chapters is not given to many. Even if you have such an ability, you need something more. In the midst of the most interesting of lives are dull bits of routine, undramatic incidents, daily boredoms; the author, when he gives birth to his book inside him, has to be an editor as well, knowing what to leave out, what to highlight, how to present his material so as to make the most of it.

It is true that some authors, particularly in America, depend very heavily on their publishers' editors to supply the spelling, the grammar, the general editing and sometimes even the background research for their books. I don't particularly approve of this. But at least one usually has to admit that such writers have one great God-given talent—they are mostly superb story-tellers, and though I still feel that a good author should not depend on others for technique, much can be forgiven the man who can enthral us with his narrative powers.

Mr. Worthington, it is just remotely possible that I am mistaken about your abilities. Thirty years of experience tell me that I am not. Thirty years of experience have also brought me to believe that the only 'mute, inglorious Miltons' around are those who want to remain mute and inglorious. Real ability will out, whatever discouragement it is given initially. So if you do happen to be a Milton, I can feel pretty certain that this letter won't stifle your talent.

Yours sincerely,

P.S. You, Mr. Worthington, a Milton? I've got to be joking!

21

Dear Sir,

It is with great regret that I have to tell you that we appear to have lost your typescript. I cannot apologise adequately for this appalling carelessness.

It is some consolation to me to know that this is only the second such loss in the twenty years that I have been in charge of this department, and during that time we have handled something between fifteen and twenty thousand books and typescripts of all sorts.

We keep a register of all books which are submitted to us, and normally we know where each one is at any stage during its consideration. In this unfortunate case, I can only assume that your typescript was underneath another one and that the two typescripts were sent back to the author of the book which was on top. If that is so, there is a good chance that your book will be returned to us shortly.

In common with the practice of most publishers, the printed slip which we use to acknowledge receipt of a book submitted for our consideration carries a statement to the effect that we cannot be held responsible for the loss or damage of books or typescripts while they are in our possession. Nevertheless, we would be very willing, assuming that you hold a carbon copy of the typescript, to pay for it to be photocopied as a replacement for the lost copy. If you have a handwritten copy of the book only, we would make a contribution to the cost of retyping it, and if this is the case, may I suggest that you should have at least two carbon copies made? Then, in the unlikely event that the same sort of thing should occur again, if would be less of a disaster.

Again my most humble apologies.

Yours truly,

22

Dear Douglas,

I am terribly sorry to have to send your new book back, with the sad news that we don't want to make an offer for it.

Let me hasten to say that I enjoyed it as much as anything of yours that I've read, and admired as always the expertise you demonstrate and the neatness of the plot and the excitement of the climax.

So what is wrong with it? Only the fact that this genre of novel has gone out of favour recently. People no longer seem willing to buy this kind of book, perhaps because they had a surfeit of them a few years ago when they were all the rage.

Publishers try to be very conscious of trends of this sort, but one of their problems is that because it takes time to publish a book they often bring out new titles when the demand for that category of book is on the wane. This is, of course, what has happened to us and it makes us even more wary than we might otherwise have been of a book like yours.

Naturally, by turning the book down I automatically free you of all obligations to us, and you are very welcome to offer the book elsewhere. You may possibly find another publisher who thinks differently, or who is so anxious to get you on his list that he will take the book, even though we are basically right about it.

Please think it over carefully. What I would like you to do is to put it on one side, and think about a new book. Let me know what you have in mind—use my knowledge, such as it is, of trends and of ideas that are doomed before they start. I may well be able to save you months of fruitless labour on a book in an out-of-fashion genre, or I might even suggest a book that I would like you to write for us. In other words, don't shut yourself into a tower as you write.

I shall look forward anxiously to your reply. I hope that we may continue the very happy relationship that we have enjoyed over the past couple of years. That sounds very pompous and formal, I'm afraid. It's not easy to tell a fine writer that he's gone off the the tracks, and it's making me nervous—hence the pomposity.

Forgive me, and let me know what you feel about this letter.

Yours ever,

23

Dear David,

Of course I understand that you would like to send your book elsewhere. Since I have rejected it, you are entirely free to do so—and perhaps you are right, too, because editors are just as fallible as anybody else, and I may have made a ghastly mistake. I have to stick to my decision, though it may well be that in future years I shall have to add your book to my list of the big ones that got away. (All publishers will occasionally swap sad stories of the great best-sellers that they were foolish enough to turn down.)

Do try someone else. The other day a publisher friend gave me a copy of a new book of his. 'Hilarious,' he said. 'Absolutely marvellous. If I don't sell ten thousand, I'll give up.' I thought the book was abysmal, and the unfunniest thing I had read in years. I wouldn't have expected to sell ten copies. So you see, we don't all think alike. Good thing, too.

If you fail to sell the book elsewhere, please, please come back with your next one. I promise not to say: 'I told you so'.

Yours,

24

Dear Owen,

Thank you for your letter.

Yes, it is quite true that all the criticisms I made of your last book when I rejected it can fairly be levelled against at least two of the books we recently published.

It is a confusing situation for an author. One of the reasons why it comes about is that between the time that a book is bought and its actual publication, one's policies can change. They frequently do change, and we find ourselves committed to books which we no longer wish to publish. It is however usually cheaper in the end to bring them out than to cancel the contract (because by the time the decision against publishing is made one has normally incurred considerable costs—if one goes ahead, one has some chance of recouping at least a part of them, but if one abandons the book, one loses everything one has spent), but this may mislead an author who is looking carefully at the publisher's books to see whether his own work is suitable for that list.

The other point is, of course, that we publishers are human and erratic and subject to influences and pressures. I don't think it is true of me in the two cases you mention, but I know that I have bought books because I liked the author, or I had a sudden enthusiasm for the subject of the book, or because it was a beautiful day; and I have rejected them because everyone in the office has been crabby all morning, or because it was raining, or because I personally suddenly got bored with the subject of the book.

This hit-or-miss method of selection doesn't happen all that often, and cannot do so if there is a really strong policy in the firm which would affect the book in question. If we decided, for instance, not to publish any more crime books, I couldn't be seduced into signing more up because of some trivial outside influence. But policies are frequently much less rigid than that, and it is then that editors can take the unexpected line, simply because they are as irrational as anyone else in the world.

I'm sorry not to be able to change my mind about your book. The rejection is in fact entirely on the grounds that we are not having any success with that category of book at the present time, and the two similar books which you mention only go to prove this point.

I hope that this letter helps to clarify the matter for you. If you do decide to put the book away and start work on a new one, I shall be most grateful, and shall look forward to discussing it with you as soon as you're ready to do so.

Yours,

25

Dear Mr. Jameson,

My good friend Arthur Harris had spoken to me about you, so your letter was expected, and there was no need to apologise for bothering me—I just hope I can help.

After reading all you have to say about your present publisher I am not surprised that you feel discontented. You are certainly treated in a somewhat offhand way and I can understand after the personal effort that you have put into the promotion of your books that you feel the publisher is not really doing his fair share. On the other hand, the sales figures you quote are quite impressive.

I'd like to put one or two points to you:

1. All publishers are inefficient to some extent or other, simply because they and their staffs are human and subject to carelessness, forgetfulness, laziness, stupidity and all the other deficiencies which make us less than gods. (Incidentally, the general use of computers seems to have aggravated these faults!)

2. No publisher is uninterested in selling his books. It may appear that way, but it does him no good to have the books sitting in his warehouse, and though some of us may seem a little more complacent than others about the speed with which they move out of that warehouse, we are all basically in the business to sell books and thus to make money for ourselves and for our authors.

3. Except in the very rare cases where publishers also own a bookshop or two, the publisher just cannot force the retailer to order his books or to re-order if he sells out.

4. Most publishers find it difficult to decide just how much good publicity and promotion does. And they are all aware that it eats at a remarkably fast rate into the profits.

5. Any publisher achieving the kind of sales you mention may find it very easy to rest on his laurels, and devote more of his energies to selling those books on his list which are not doing nearly so well.

All those points deal with question of sales and promotion. Now let us look at the more personal matters.

Your complaint that you get no editorial help from your present publisher is, I think, a frequent cause of dissatisfaction—at least among English authors. If you were American, you might be complaining that you receive too much help! Certainly on this side of the Atlantic a great many editors seem either unwilling or unable to advise their authors. But I sometimes wonder whether this is partly the authors' fault, because so many of them resent any criticism, however valid and constructive. Have you actually discussed this point with your publisher? You might find that he is only holding back from diffidence or uncertainty about your reaction.

Perhaps you haven't been able to talk to him about it, because I see you say that he is apparently reluctant to spare much time or attention for you. It is possible however that he is giving you the maximum he can manage in this direction. I'd like to state here what I consider to be one of the great unrealised truths about publisher-author relationships: *one of the most difficult things in the whole complex business is for the author to understand that his book is one thirtieth (or even one three-hundredth) of the publisher's year; and it is equally difficult for the publisher to remember constantly that this book, one of thirty (or three hundred) that he is publishing during the next twelve months, represents a whole year (or three years, or twenty years) of the author's working life*. If we could all bear that in mind at all times, one of the greatest barriers to understanding and happy working together of publishers and authors would disappear.

One of the things that makes author-publisher relationships more difficult is a general assumption that since we are all in the word business we are all expert communicators. In fact, of course, many authors who can communicate perfectly in their books are inarticulate in conversation and even in letters do not write with the clarity that they employ in their work. Publishers are not much better than any other businessmen at expressing exactly what they mean.

Is the neglect that you feel a matter therefore of the publisher being too busy? Or of him not being aware of what you need because you have failed to communicate with each other? Or is it possible that you demand too much from him, either by expecting perfection or by constantly complaining, or both?

Perhaps I have wasted a lot of my time and yours in this letter, because the whole problem may simply be one of personality. When an author has his book accepted by a publisher, he usually does not know the editor who is going to be his main contact in the firm, and when he does get to know him he may find that one or both members of the partnership are not compatible. If this is the case, why don't you ask whether there is someone else in the business who could look after you and your books? It may be difficult to bring yourself to say this, but if your relationship with the man is already poor, you can't make it much worse, and you might find that the result is a new and happy friendship.

May I ask you to think about some of the things I have set down in this excessively long letter? If you still feel that you must change your publisher, give my secretary a ring and fix an appointment to come in and see me, and we can talk the whole thing over and I will see what I can do to help you find a more congenial home.

Yours sincerely,

26

To an author who writes to say that he wishes to move to another publisher

Dear Richard,

As you will have expected I was very unhappy indeed to read your letter.

Of course I will release you from your contract, much as it grieves me to do so. Even if we were to continue our past arguments about our abilities as far as your books are concerned, and even if I were able to convince you that we are not entirely to blame for your disappointments, the fact remains that you have lost confidence in us and are no longer happy on our list. I would hate to force an author to stick to his contract under such circumstances. I know some publishers go on for years bringing out books by authors with whom they are barely on speaking terms, but it seems very curious to me, for I believe that there must be mutual trust and respect and friendship between author and publisher.

Thank you for all that has been good in our past relationship, and good luck with your new publisher. I shall pounce eagerly on your new books as they appear and be proud to say: 'yes, I published his first book.'

Yours ever,

27

Dear Mr. Wilcock,

I am sorry to have kept you waiting so long for a verdict on your book. Unfortunately I still haven't got a complete answer for you. At the moment your book is going through various processes to determine whether or not it is an economic proposition for us.

That means of course that we like it. It has been considered editorially and we're all enthusiastic. But don't count on anything yet. You see, publishing is a business nowadays. It is not enough to like a book—one has to be sure that one is also going to make money from publishing it.

This commercial attitude is widespread among publishers these days, but it hasn't always been so. A friend of mine in hardcover publishing told me recently that until a few years ago their method was to find a book they liked, think of a number and print it, think of a price and charge it, and look at the balance sheet at the end of the year to see whether they had been right or wrong. This is a somewhat distorted account of their procedures, because they certainly prepared estimates of a sort for the books they published, but at the same time it is true that much of their business was conducted in an undisciplined way. Even then that is not quite so irresponsible as it may sound, because those apparently wild guesses at print quantities and price were based on many years of experience, and were in fact informed guesses.

But, my friend went on to say, the firm no longer operated in that slightly haphazard way. Every book was costed out before it was accepted, and if it did not show an immediate profit on the quantity that it could realistically be expected to sell, then it would not be published by that firm, without some other very special reason for taking it on. This might be, for instance, that the book was a minor work by a well-established author—but even then the publishers would be a lot more wary about it than in the past.

You see, we're in business to make money. This sometimes seems to surprise people, who expect plumbers and boot manufacturers and airlines to want to show a profit on their work, but are faintly taken aback at the thought that publishers should want to eat too. Oh, I know that occasionally we will publish a book knowing that we shall lose money on it—this is because we feel a duty every now and then to do something for Literature or for a charity that we are interested in. But that sort of publishing is becoming rarer, and it's getting harder and harder for authors to get their books published, and they're having to become more and more professional as a result.

It's true of everything—there's little room in the modern world for amateurs.

Anyway, Mr. Wilcock, I am glad you wrote, because it has given me the opportunity of explaining the delay and also of saying that I thought your book was very professional in its approach. I only hope the figures we produce will allow me to make you an offer to publish it. I shall write again in a day or so from now.

Yours sincerely,

28

To an author who suggests that I should publish his book as a paperback original (i.e. without it appearing in hardcover form first)

Dear Mr. Black,

I was very interested in your proposition. As you say, there are certainly some advantages in this method of publishing—particularly the fact that you don't have to share paperback royalties with the hardcover publisher, and may therefore end up considerably better off financially.

I would be willing to consider your book on this basis, but before I do I should like to point out that there are also several important disadvantages to this procedure.

First of all, you may lose prestige. Perhaps this is not important to you, but there is something about a hardcover book which gives an author a stature or status symbol that a paperback (even if it has that celebrated bird as its imprint) cannot really equal.

Secondly, you will have less chance of good reviews. Few newspapers devote as much space to new paperbacks as they do to hardcover books.

Thirdly, many hardcover firms have a much wider range of products than a paperback concern, and this may be of use to you at some stage or other if you decide to write a different kind of book.

Fourthly, if you remain with a hardcover house you have at least two editors—the hardcover one and me. Which may or may not be an advantage!

However, having said all that, I should point out that in common with most paperback firms we are closely associated with a hardcover house. We work closely together, and although we do not issue paperbacks of all their books, nor they hardcovers of all our originals, many books appear on both lists, and if I thought your book would interest my hardcover friends I would certainly show it to them. If they took it, you would have another advantage in that you would get the full paperback royalty.

So send me your book, and let us take it from there.

Yours sincerely,

29

To an author who asks advice on whether to employ an agent

Dear Mr. Finnegan,

I was glad to know from your letter that in principle you were prepared to accept my offer for your book. I do not think you are 'foolish or lacking in gratitude' because you are considering going to an agent and seeking his advice about the offer. On the contrary, I think you're very wise.

I have no doubt at all that many publishers would advise you against using an agent. This isn't because they want to cheat those authors that they sign up direct—on the whole publishers are fairly honest. However they are perfectly prepared to send to authors who do not have professional advisers contracts which are slightly less favourable to the authors than the kind of agreements which literary agents would insist on. Let me make it quite clear that the differences are minor—no good publisher sets out to exploit an unsuspecting author—but they do exist.

Now if you go to a literary agent you will have to pay him ten per cent of the monies that your book earns (and a rather higher percentage on foreign sales in most cases—because an agent in the foreign country concerned has also been involved in the deal, and he needs to live too, so he has to have a piece of the action).

What do you get in return for your ten per cent? First of all, you are employing an expert in the market. A literary agent knows which publishers are looking for books of a certain type and which are not (many authors waste an awful lot of time and money by sending their typescripts to the wrong publisher); he knows the going rate for books, so that he can tell whether a publisher's offer is an entirely fair one or not; he is expert too in selling other rights—translation, film, serial rights, and so on—which the publisher is sometimes good at and sometimes not, and again he knows the market prices for such sales; he can understand publishers' contracts and tell you whether you can safely sign or whether there is something unfair hidden away in the small type; he can advise and help you in a number of other ways—for instance, most agents have considerable literary skill, understand quite a lot about the tax laws as they affect authors, and frequently find themselves acting as friends and counsellors to authors in all sorts of matters which are not directly related to the business of writing and selling literary properties; he can collect monies for you if your publisher should be dilatory in paying; in short, he can relieve you of all the problems of marketing your work and looking after the business side of being an author.

Perhaps one of the most important parts of an agent's job, and this is particularly why I like my authors to have an agent, is to act as an intermediary in any dispute between the author and the publisher or in any matter which either side finds embarrassing to discuss directly with the other. The relationship between author and publisher is all too often a pretty delicate plant, which can easily be destroyed by a quite minor disagreement, but if the matter can be discussed through a third party whom both author and publisher respect, relationships can often be successfully preserved. The agent, of course, is not entirely unbiased—he represents the author, so he is on the author's side—but at same time, the good agent also understands the publisher's point of view, and a fair verdict or settlement can often therefore be reached.

By the way, I should perhaps make it clear that agents do not normally take any money from the author until the author's literary property brings in money. The majority of agents do not make a charge for reading a typescript or for submitting it unsuccessfully to a publisher. They charge once they have produced some money for you.

So, Mr. Finnegan, do by all means employ an agent. You will find a list of agents in *Cassell's Directory of Publishing* or in *The Writers' and Artists' Year Book* (which, incidentally, gives full details of many of the percentages they charge on overseas sales). Both of these books should be available at your public library. I would be happy to make a recommendation if you like, or to leave the choice to you.

Yours sincerely,

30

To an author who asks if I will alter my offer from an advance against royalties to an outright payment

Dear John Austin,

Thanks for your letter and your basic acceptance of my offer to publish your book.

I do understand and sympathise with your motive in asking for an outright payment. You are not the first author, and I'm sure you won't be the last, to find himself in a situation in which you feel that a lump sum of £5,000 would be of more value to you at this moment in time than an advance of £1,500 against royalties.

I'm very sorry, but I'm not going to agree. I absolutely deplore the idea of outright payments for copyright. They are so rarely fair. Either the publisher pays more for the book than it is worth (this doesn't happen often, and when it does I would not weep over much, because the publisher ought to know better and can probably afford it anyway—but even so, I think it is wrong) or the author undersells himself. This latter situation may not matter very much if the difference between the outright payment and the sum the book would otherwise have earned is small, but suppose the book becomes a steady seller, suppose film rights are sold, suppose the property goes on increasing in value (as sometimes happens), and the author gets nothing except that initial payment, which may have looked handsome at the time, but which now looks incredibly mean. Of course, the publisher can always make a voluntary payment to make up for the fact that the author is now reaping no reward, but his auditors will want to know how such a course is justified from the business point of view.

No, my friend, I may not always offer top sums, high royalties, full shares of subsidiary rights, but I will always offer something fair and never, never do an outright deal.

The one exception to this is the case of anthologies, where it is simpler and reasonably fair to make an outright payment for the use of the story or poem or extract concerned. Even then, I feel it is not unreasonable if I am asked to pay an additional sum if I reprint the book.

I have one suggestion to make. Since I am fairly confident that the book will earn quite a lot more than £1,500, I will increase the proposed advance to £2,500. I can't go the whole hog to the £5,000 you want, because that would increase my risk beyond a point that I am willing to accept. Even £2,500 is more than I want to pay, especially with money being tight, but I hope it may solve some of your difficulties.

Yours sincerely,

31

Dear Ronald,

I do understand how you feel about a synopsis—many other authors find them equally difficult to set down on paper and believe too, as you do, that writing a synopsis is a pretty useless exercise because, once the actual writing begins, the plot and characters and practically everything about the book may change so radically as to bear little resemblance to the original summary.

Nevertheless, there are reasons why I still want to persuade you to put something on paper about the story.

Firstly, I maintain that however unrealistic the synopsis, the author must gain something from setting his ideas down in an orderly fashion.

Secondly, there is no need to think that anyone is going to hold you rigidly to what you have written in the summary. Any publisher recognises that authors need freedom in this respect, and the phenomenon of the characters taking control of the author and dictating the course of the book is something that we have all heard about so often that we are quite prepared for it to happen.

Thirdly, if you are asking a publisher to put out his money, I think it's only fair that you should give him something to go on. The fact that you may deviate from it very substantially at a later stage of the writing is immaterial. In the meantime at least your editor has a piece of paper to wave at his bosses and his sales colleagues when they ask what the new Ronald Wilborn book is about.

Fourthly, though I beg you to believe that I am not going to interfere, I do think there is something to be gained by letting me see the synopsis before you start work so that I can make any comments that occur to me. If those comments turn out to be irrelevant, you're entirely at liberty to ignore them. On the other hand I might come up with a bright idea which you could use or which might save you some wasted time.

Do please think it over.

Yours,

P.S. If I were dealing with a new author to our list, and a comparatively inexperienced one, I should probably be asking for a synopsis of some 3,000 to 4,000 words, which would obviously go into a great deal of detail. That's not necessary in your case, because I know your work and capabilities so well. A couple of pages will do—a bare outline of the plot. OK?

32

Dear Barry,

I have just finished reading your synopsis for the new novel and am writing at once to say that though I think it's a marvellous story it terrifies me out of my wits!

I am not a libel expert, but it seems to me that this book-to-be is absolutely riddled with libel possibilities. The big problem is that if you take a real organisation like the Coal Board, and actually name it in the book, then all the members of that organisation can claim that they are identified with the characters who hold the same office in your book. However much you may alter the physical characteristics of, for instance, the Chairman, however many disclaimers you put in the book to say that your Chairman is not in any way based on, or meant to be a representation of the real Chairman, if you write anything which, if it applied to the real Chairman, might be construed as damaging to him, then he can sue you.

Libel is one of the most frightening of the disasters that can hit a publisher. You see, not only can he lose large sums of money in damages (which, despite the fact that the author has given him an indemnity clause, he often cannot recover from the author simply because the poor chap isn't wealthy enough), but he can also lose the entire edition of the book and all the costs involved in its production, let alone the lost profit. Some publishers carry insurance against libel, but it is very expensive and usually does not cover all the possible loss involved.

Of course, the legal costs of defending an action for obscene libel are just as great, but normally in such cases the publisher feels he has a moral duty to fight against what he regards as censorship. Besides, he has more often than not been conscious of the risk from the beginning—he has gone into the whole thing with his eyes open. But the only person in many cases of ordinary libel or defamation of character or whatever the legal jargon may be who can really advise the publisher as to the dangers of what has been written is the author himself—and often the author does not have the necessary legal knowledge to understand the matter anyway.

In this case, it is quite clear to me that there is a substantial danger. It may be that the book would not finally be libellous at all. This depends on what you write about the various identifiable characters. It is a matter for an expert. Can you consult a really good solicitor on this point? If necessary, and it might be the best idea anyway, I could arrange for you to have a discussion with our own legal advisers, who are expert in all matters to do with publishing and specialists in questions of libel.

I am sorry to write like this. I think all publishers get a little hysterical about libel. Accuse me of publishing pornography, burn down our warehouse, tell me I have printed a book back to front, prove that I no longer hold any rights in the book that I have just re-issued—at the news of any of these horrors I shall remain reasonably calm; but tell me that I am to be sued for libel, and my blood runs cold and I ask my secretary to book me on the next plane for South America.

Please be careful.

Yours tremblingly,

P.S. The potential printers of the book join me in this plea. They, who are really only our servants, printing what we ask them to print, are held equally responsible when there is trouble of this kind. You see how the dangers mount up.

33

To an author who asks how I see my role as editor of the novel he wishes to write and which I propose to commission

Dear Steve,

Thank you for your letter.

For a lot of the time an editor (and this is particularly true of those who work for paperback houses) is a selector, choosing which books his firm will publish, but not altering, except perhaps in a very minor way, their content. He does this with existing typescripts and specially of course with American books which are frequently in print by the time the British editor sees them. It is an interesting job. Even more interesting is the work of an editor when he is actually involved in the writing of a book. I believe that an editor has a great deal to contribute to the process, primarily because it is extremely difficult for an author, or any artist for that matter, to judge his own work. The editor acts as a critic, but he is sympathetic to the author's aims and ideas, and if he's good at his job he knows something of the techniques of writing and the demands of the market, and so his criticisms are informed and constructive and may even give the author inspiration.

In America, publishers' editors play a very dominant role in their relationships with authors, and while some of the latter are happy to have their books virtually rewritten by an editor (one sometimes wonders whose name should appear on the book!), others find the interference intolerable. On the other hand, British editors seem to me on the whole far too timid and reluctant to offer advice. The happy medium is somewhere in between, and that's what I shall try to provide.

How I provide it depends very largely on you, and your methods of working. You see, I know perfectly well that some authors cannot bear to discuss their work, let alone show it to anyone, until it is finished (and incidentally the more strongly they feel about a particular person the more difficult they may find it to show the book to that person—it's often easier to give it to a complete stranger to read than to one's wife, for example). Others are willing to reveal everything, right from the synopsis stage. I don't know how you feel about such matters, but whatever your neuroses, I will respect them. It doesn't matter to me, and I wouldn't dream of trying to alter your methods—but it does affect my work. Obviously if I can't see the book until you have finished it, I shall have to reserve all comments until then—and if I'm very unhappy with the draft you show me, this may make for a somewhat difficult situation, since you may not want to start all over again, or make basic alterations. However, if that's the way you work, that's the way it will have to be. On the other hand, if you can bear to show me things at an earlier stage, then I can make comments as we go along, and you will know that I am happy about the book, or if I am not, we shall try to solve the problems.

There's an important point on that score, incidentally. When we meet problems and try to solve them together, we may find ourselves in considerable disagreement. I can tell you here and now that you will win every argument. I shall certainly fight hard for my point of view, but in the final analysis the book is yours, not mine—you are the creative artist, not I—and I shall never force you to make a change against your will. All I ask is that you listen as carefully to my comments as I shall to yours.

Perhaps I can take that last point a stage farther. Since the author is the only begetter of the book it is really best for the editor if he pokes his nose in only when the author invites him to do so and even then does so with the utmost diffidence. The problem this raises of course is that the author isn't always aware of exactly when he needs help. But let me underline it—modesty becomes an editor, and good editors exist only because of good writers.

I suppose the whole thing could be summed up very briefly really: as your editor I shall try to be whatever you want me to be—adviser, sounding-board, critic, comforter, shoulder-to-weep-on, inspirer, friend. It's not an easy role, and I can't guarantee to perform it adequately. I can only tell you that it's not as difficult as your own job as an author.

Yours,

34

Dear Mr. Pollard,

I wonder whether there is any possibility that you could travel to London within the next week or two so that we could meet and discuss various matters about your book.

I should have asked you this when I first wrote to say that we should like to publish it, but I'm afraid I got tied up in explaining the intricacies of our contract, and it slipped my mind. My apologies.

I hope you won't read anything dire into this suggestion of a meeting. It is simply that I think it is most important that we should have some direct contact and not depend solely on letters and the occasional telephone call. There's nothing like face-to-face discussion for getting things really straight, and also once you've talked to a person in the flesh it is less easy to misunderstand what he means when he writes or phones.

I envy you your beautiful and quiet surroundings on Exmoor, but though there is a definite advantage for authors to live away from the hustle and distractions of the city, there are some dangers.

Let me give you two examples. An author I know was commissioned to write a novel. He sent in the first twenty thousand words, which the publisher liked tremendously, but in which he saw a few minor flaws. He wrote back to the author trying to convey both his enthusiasm and the minor criticisms. The author completely misunderstood the letter and nearly gave up writing the book altogether, because he was convinced that the publisher hated it. It really wasn't a case of an ambiguous letter or a dim-witted interpretation of it—it all happened because the author didn't know the publisher and hadn't fully understood what he saw as his editorial function.

The second instance happened to me. An author completed his book and sent it to me to read. I was delighted with it, but when talking to him on the telephone about it, I merely said: 'It'll do!' I was grinning at the time, but my author couldn't see the smile, didn't realise that I was pleased, thought I was merely trying to cover up my disappointment, and nearly burst into tears as a result. It took a lot of words before he could be convinced that his interpretation was wrong.

I am sure we shall be able to avoid these misunderstandings anyway, but a meeting would undoubtedly help us to do so.

I shall look forward to hearing from you.

Yours sincerely,

35

Dear Mary,

Don't worry about the way I finish my letters. There is a curious convention in the publishing world which decrees that as soon as you are on first name terms with anybody in it—publishers, agents, authors—you sign off your letters to the person concerned with the one word 'Yours'. Not 'Yours sincerely' or 'Yours very truly' or anything else. Just 'Yours'. Or possibly 'Yours ever'.

Don't be misled. This is a pure formality and does not imply any deep affection or even an attempt to seduce you into undue familiarity. I know perfectly well that I am not yours, nor are you mine. So put it down simply as another absurdity of publishing when I sign myself:

Yours,

36

Dear George,

Herewith at last the contract for your book.

Since it is your first publisher's contract, perhaps I had better go through one or two points in it.

I think the first controversial issue is where it says that if you do not deliver the typescript by the prescribed date the publisher may decline to publish the work. This clause is not normally invoked unless the book is of a desperately topical nature or the author is incredibly late in delivering the typescript. Naturally any publisher likes a book to be delivered on time, but he is usually very sympathetic to unavoidable delays, and will frequently extend the delivery date by a very long time—providing that it is genuinely necessary, and of course if the author has taken the trouble to consult the publisher and inform him of the problems which may delay delivery.

'The Author is required to bear the cost of alterations to the proofs apart from printer's errors in excess of 10% of the cost of composition.' The point here is that sometimes authors take the opportunity of completely rewriting their books at proof stage. The publisher shouldn't have to pay for such rewriting; the author should get his book right in the first place, and then it wouldn't be necessary. Alterations required because of the book having become out of date, or because new information has been discovered between it being written and set in type—these are a different kettle of fish, and the publisher will probably be very sympathetic about them.

The warranty clause, in which the author guarantees the originality, ownership and freedom of illegal content (e.g. libel) of his work, is frequently a cause of contention. I feel it is entirely justified from the publisher's point of view, and would beg any author to read it carefully and consider what he is signing. If he is in doubt about it, he should consult the publisher, or a solicitor, or both.

The territory clause. This is often a very mysterious thing for authors, I find. Let me try to explain. For publishers of English language books the world, like all Gaul, is divided into three parts. These are the traditional British market (roughly equivalent to the British Commonwealth), the United States of America and its dependencies and the Philippine Republic, and the rest of the world (or Open market). Now frequently an English language publisher will buy world rights in a book, but in many cases either the American rights have already been sold or there is a commitment on them, or perhaps an agent is involved and will not sell the American rights to the British publisher. In any of those cases the British publisher is likely to have for English language editions an exclusive licence to publish the book in the traditional British market, and a non-exclusive licence to publish the book in the Open market. He won't be able to publish his book at all in the U.S.A. (because that territory already belongs or will belong exclusively to an American publisher), but equally the American publisher won't be able to sell his edition of the book in the British market. On the continent of Europe, and in South America and various other (mostly non-English-speaking) parts of the world, both the British and American publishers will have a non-exclusive licence, so they will both be able to sell their English language editions of the book in that market at the same time and in competition with one another. I said earlier that the traditional British market was roughly the same as the British Commonwealth—it would be truer to say that it is much the same as the Commonwealth was just after World War II, for the fact that certain countries have left the Commonwealth and become independent has not removed them from the British publisher's traditional market, though they are no longer officially Commonwealth members. There is one other confusing complication in this matter of exclusive and non-exclusive markets, and that is the question of Canada. If the book is of British origin Canada is usually included in the British publisher's exclusive territory; if it is of American origin Canada is usually included in the U.S. publisher's exclusive territory; occasionally, just to make matters more difficult, Canada becomes a non-exclusive market.

If you have understood that last inordinately long paragraph (well done!), I have to tell you that the situation has become even more labyrinthine in recent years. Exclusive British rights nowadays do not always include all the territories of the old British Empire—Australian rights may be withheld, for example—and the 1992

Common Market regulations are likely to result in further changes, all of which means that the exclusive and open market territories may vary from contract to contract.

Royalties. You will see that there are all kinds of royalty payments apart from the basic percentage on the published price. This happens largely because the publisher has many methods of selling his books, and in some cases what he receives for them does not relate directly to the published price, or is so much less than the 'normal' return that a reduced royalty payment is justified.

Subsidiary rights. There are many of these, but you will see that they fall into two sections: those which the author grants to the publisher (subject to the payment of certain percentages of any monies the publisher receives for them), and those of which the author retains control but which he allows the publisher (again in exchange for various percentages) to negotiate on his behalf. The difference between them is really that the first batch falls under the general heading of 'volume rights'—this is what a publisher expects to purchase when he buys the rights in a book; the second batch is less directly concerned with publishing in book form, such as film and television rights. The various percentages payable on subsidiary rights are, in most publishers' contracts, those recommended by the Publishers Association.

The advance payment. You requested that I should make this money payable as to half the sum on signature of the Agreement by both parties and half on delivery of the typescript. I'm afraid I cannot agree to this, and, talking to my colleagues in the publishing business, I find that fewer and fewer of them can afford nowadays to make the payments in this way. What I have put in is a third of the money on signature of the Agreement, a third on delivery of a complete and satisfactory typescript and a third on publication. I hope you will agree.

You will note the words 'a complete and satisfactory typescript'. I don't suppose for a moment that it would happen in your case, but it could turn out that a delivered typescript needed an awful lot of reworking, and I think the publisher should have the chance of being completely satisfied before paying out more money. This method also provides a 'carrot' with which to induce the author to undertake any necessary revisions. The Society of Authors and Writers' Guild of Great Britain might argue that the wording is little better than the so-called 'acceptance' clause which frequently appears in Agreements, when the second part of the advance is payable 'on acceptance' by the publisher of the typescript. They say that such a clause invalidates the contract to publish, leaving the publisher committed only to considering the typescript for publication at delivery stage, and free to reject it arbitrarily. I assure you that our commitment goes beyond that, and I hope that you will find the wording acceptable (it appears in many agented contracts, by the way).

Another point about the advance is that it is on account of all monies received by us under the contract; in other words, if we receive some money for, say, the French translation rights in the book, you will not receive your share of that money until the advance has been earned by all the forms of cash—royalties on our sales, or advances against foreign publishers' sales, or whatever it may be—that we have received. The question of when payments, other than the advance, are made sometimes gives rise to quite a lot of bad feeling. For example, it may happen that before the book has been published, enough money has been earned from subsidiary rights to cover the advance and that there is in fact money owing to the author. Some publishers will insist on keeping this money until the first accounting date after publication of their edition of the book. Their contracts entitle them to do this, but it is a practice of which I personally disapprove.

You will see that you may give us notice to re-issue or reprint the book within nine months, if it is not available for sale, and that if we fail to comply with this notice the rights may revert to you. I hope we don't get to such a position, but if we do, I would ask that you should discuss the matter with me before sending in your formal notice. I will promise not to hang on to rights that I am not going to use, but there are sometimes reasons for not allowing rights to revert immediately they are asked for (a plan to reprint in twelve months' time, for instance) and I'd like the chance of putting such reasons to you if in fact they exist.

The option clause is another that can cause great disagreement—at least it used to do so some years ago. Nowadays it is usually so innocuous that no one really objects to it, because it merely says that the publisher shall have the opportunity of seeing the author's next book. Since it does not mention specific terms (in the past option clauses frequently said that the new book could be signed up by the publisher on the same terms as the book under contract—and that was often very unfair to the author), but refers to 'terms which shall be fair and reasonable', both parties are in fact left very free, since the interpretation of 'fair and reasonable' may be totally different according to which side you are on. It seems only just that the publisher should have the opportunity of seeing the author's next book—after all, he may have spent a great deal of time and money on the first one, and may have achieved a considerable success for it and its author—but after that the whole matter is open to negotiation.

The Society of Authors and the Writers' Guild are all for deleting option clauses altogether. Perhaps they are right. Cut the clause out if you like, and I'll simply hope to earn the chance of seeing your next book by doing well with this one.

I'm afraid this is a very long letter, and I have only touched on some of the questions which arise more frequently. If there are points that you want clarified, please don't hesitate to ask. A publisher's contract is a pretty complex legal document. Most publishers have evolved their forms of contract over a period of years, using a great deal of professional advice, both from fellow publishers and from their legal advisers, so it's not really surprising if you don't understand everything at first reading. And if you are still worried after my explanations, please go to the Society of Authors or the Writers' Guild or to an agent or to a solicitor who specialises in this kind of agreement.

One of the things which seems to have happened in the publishing world since the last war is that unfairnesses have largely disappeared. Most publishers behave honourably towards their authors—which certainly could not have been so confidently said in the pre-war days. Nevertheless, an agreement which may be perfectly fair in most circumstances, may not necessarily be so in an individual case, so if there is anything that worries you, please say so.

I shall look forward to hearing from you in due course. If you find the agreement acceptable, would you please initial it where I have marked it and sign it at the bottom of the last page, and then return it to me. I will then send you a counterpart, initialled and signed by me in the same places. I shall also enclose our cheque for the first part of the advance.

Yours,

37

Dear Danny,

Thanks for your letter.

I don't think there's any real necessity for an author to join any organisation. On the other hand, though it may not be essential, it's probably a very good thing to do.

There are several societies (they are listed in *The Writers' and Artists' Yearbook* and in *The Writer's Handbook*), some specialist and some general. The Society of Authors and the Writer's Guild of Great Britain are particularly useful for an author without professional advice, for they supply this, together with legal and other services. Both the Society and the Guild are trade unions; the Guild is affiliated to the T.U.C., but the Society is not. Organisations like the Crime Writers Association and the Romantic Novelists Association are of course for specialists only. The Book Trust (which used to be called the National Book League) is obviously A Good Thing, and—well, look at the lists for yourself.

As well as national and international organisations, there are literary societies in most towns. Some are good and some are ghastly, and you'll just have to find out which variety your local one is. The public library can probably tell you when and where they meet and who the secretary is.

The main point about these societies and organisations, it seems to me, is that they provide authors with a chance of meeting their fellows and of comparing notes with them and discovering that they all suffer from the same kinds of trials and tribulations in their dealings with wicked publishers. Several of the organisations provide various services—advice to members, pension funds, research facilities, and so on.

Not a real necessity, but worth doing—if you can afford it, because of course they all charge membership fees.

Yours,

38

Dear Tony,

I am sending herewith a contract for the as yet untitled novel about smuggling in the eighteenth century in Cornwall. I think you will find everything in order, but please don't hesitate to write if there is anything you want to question in it.

One matter I have some doubts about, and that is the delivery date for the typescript. I have put in 'March 31st' because most writers seem to like a deadline to work to and this seems a possible date for completion. If it gives you too little time, by all means alter it. Since the book is not topical, it honestly does not make a great deal of difference to me whether it is available in March or in September. Had it been one of those books designed to tie in with a particular date (a book about Churchill, say, to be published on the anniversary of his birth or death) or a particular event (such as the launching of a film), it would have been of considerable importance to me that you should deliver it quickly and on time. In this case however you can have some latitude. But not too much! After all, I am paying you money at the time we sign this agreement, and though it may not be a fortune, I want to start recouping that money as soon as I can. I can't begin to do so until the book is actually published, and of course the publication date cannot be fixed until the typescript is delivered.

So be a good lad and accept March 31st if you can—but if not, make it as soon after as does seem reasonable to you.

Yours,

39

Dear Rob,

Yes, please do send me the revised draft of the first twenty thousand words of the novel.

There are disadvantages in showing an editor part of a book but there are also advantages. For instance, there is the danger that the editor may make all manner of criticisms which are irrelevant and even extremely irritating simply because he does not know what happens in the rest of the book and the author does. And when the editor discovers that his comments are useless, he feels he is wasting his time, and the author is disappointed that the editor doesn't understand what he, the author, is driving at.

On the other hand, to see a novel in its early stages is often a wonderful opportunity to stop the book going wrong from the very beginning.

It's partly a matter of temperament. There are some authors who cannot bear to show anyone a single sentence of their current work until the whole thing is completed. (That's fine unless the editor dislikes the book and wants it rewritten from the beginning!) There are others who insist on showing the editor each new chapter, fresh from the typewriter. (That's ghastly, whether the book is good or bad. One author once insisted on doing that to me—he would deliver chapters at monthly intervals, and by the time a new one came in, I had forgotten the details of the earlier ones, which meant that I had to read Chapter One of that book twenty times, and Chapter Two nineteen times, and so on!) A compromise is best, and if you can show me the work at a stage when there's enough to judge but still time to make changes, and if you'll put up with any foolish comments that I make because I'm only seeing a part of the whole, then I shall be happy and I hope you will.

By the way, there's no need at all to retype your revised pages. I know you have put handwritten corrections all over them, but I'm sure I shall be able to decipher it. There's really no point in retyping until we reach final draft stage. I know we publishers make a great to-do about only considering typescripts in double spacing on one side of the paper, but that doesn't really apply when an editor is actually working with an author on a book.

I'll look forward to the draft.

Yours,

40

Dear Adrian,

I have now read the first chapters of your novel and I am tremendously impressed. The whole concept has great breadth and I am delighted with the way you have worked in so much technical information about the background so that it is not only completely comprehensible to a layman like me, but also makes fascinating reading.

BUT...

Yes, there is a very big 'but'. I think you have done this excellent work on your background and the documentary aspect of the book at the expense of the characters. I am sorry to be so blunt (as my dear friend and publisher extraordinary, the late Peter Guttmann used to say) but your characters are cardboard and dull. What is worse is that all this marvellous background material is always seen in its own terms, and never in terms of the characters and its effects on them.

I believe very firmly that the only interesting thing in the whole of life is people. I mean that very sincerely and very literally. Wild, unspoilt Highland scenery is very beautiful, but if there are no people in it it eventually becomes a bore. Science and technology, mathematics, computers all eventually become boring. Even God is a bore if He is not related to people. Everything in the world that is truly interesting is somehow connected with people.

Now, if only you can put this belief of mine into your facts and figures and your technical accuracy, then we shall have something really exciting. I have some ideas on how you can do this, so if you'd like to phone, we could discuss them.

Yours,

41

Dear Tim,

I have just read the first draft of the book. You said when you sent it that you were very unhappy about it, so let me say straight away that I think there is a great deal of terrific stuff here. Some of the action bits are very exciting, and I'm very fond of those two thugs—marvellous, warm, funny, human characters.

At the same time, I think I can see why you're dissatisfied with the book. The main trouble, in my view, is that it lacks shape. Now this is the sort of word—'shape', I mean—which sounds profound in this kind of context, but which is quite difficult to understand or to define. I think what I am talking about can, in fact, be expressed best in visual terms. I once studied play-writing, and read somewhere about the 'shape' of a three-act play being a gently ascending curve. At the end of Act One it has reached a little peak. It drops a bit then, and climbs again to a major peak at the end of Act Two. Another little drop and then a rather gentle climb to the climax just before the final curtain when everything is resolved and the tension may drop again. Can you imagine, can you *see* the kind of curve I mean? I think it applies to novels too.

And then there is another sort of shape in which you look down on the book and its plot and subplots, and they look rather like a tree, with the main trunk and the branches coming out of it—but the sort of tree where the branches curve upwards so that they mingle with and overlap the twigs on the other branches—and the whole thing makes a finished pattern, a complete entity—and it too has an upward feeling about it, so that it is finished when you get to the topmost twig of the topmost branch.

All very pretty and imaginative, but not of much practical help, you may think. Yes, I agree, but I think you have to have this kind of imagery in your mind before you can set about solving the particular problem that you are faced with. First of all, I think you should look at the book and see whether you can intensify the ascent of its curve—at the moment everything is a little flat and there isn't the tremendous tension that will raise the story to a climax and that will carry the reader on because he wants to reach that climax.

(Incidentally, I find it interesting that one uses a word like 'flat' to describe a slow, dull passage in a book. Again it is a visual approach. I suppose that all the arts have a visual quality, direct in the case of painting, sculpture, architecture, and indirect for music and writing.)

Next, look at the subplots. I think a lot can be cut, and I have marked some passages that I believe could easily go. Make sure that the subplots are truly connected with the main tree-trunk. If they're not, what are they doing in the book anyway? And do they affect each other, and link up with each other? And do they remain subplots, or are they in some cases threatening to become more important than the main trunk from which they spring?

I hope some of this is helpful. If I've been too high-flown and impractical it's because I can't entirely solve a difficulty which belongs to your creative imagination and not to my plodding critical senses.

Let me know what you feel and whether you want to try again or whether you'd rather talk about it first.

Yours,

42

Dear Martin,

I thought our meeting yesterday was very fruitful, and I shall look forward eagerly to seeing the revised draft of the novel. After you had gone I thought of a few more points I wanted to make—hence this letter.

Would you have a look at some of the names you have chosen for your characters? You have a great penchant for one-syllable names like Bond and Pike and Mead and Bain, and I must say that, since these are minor characters anyway, I began to get very confused by them. Couldn't we have some two- and three-syllable names for variety? It's surprising how much it helps to distinguish between the characters.

Again, when some of these small-part people popped up from time to time in the book, quite apart from the confusion of their names, I found it difficult to remember who they were. Could you re-identify them (very briefly, with just a word or two) when they re-appear after a long gap?

For some of the characters you have introduced characteristic speech patterns—for instance, the Chaplain's 'um' at the end of sentences, and Bill's catch-phrase—but you have tended to forget these in the second half of the book. I think they're worth keeping in because they help to identify the characters (and in a book like this with so many people mentioned by name the more aids there are to the reader's memory the better), and of course you should be consistent with them.

You have a habit of saying something such as 'the incident that followed was hilarious', or 'they were about to enter the most exciting phase of the conflict'. Well, first of all I should like you to cut these sentences altogether—if the episode is hilarious or exciting then we shall learn this in due course. But if you must keep them in, then at least look carefully at the adjectives you choose, and don't use 'hilarious' where 'amusing' would be more appropriate.

Finally, let me remind you that the essence of drama is conflict, and you need drama in a novel as much as in a play. Do let a tremendous antagonism grow up between Sean and the Doctor. It will keep the tension going and add so much more to the eventual confrontation between them.

Thanks for listening so patiently to all my suggestions yesterday. I hope these extra ones won't be the straw to the camel's back.

Yours,

43

Dear Jonathan,

I have now read the first chapters of *The Miracle Men*. I think it's very exciting indeed—in parts—but I've also got some important reservations. I hope you won't be depressed by this, because what I want to do is to encourage you and, I hope, to make some constructive criticisms. There's no reason at all to go and throw yourself off a cliff—on the contrary, you can feel very confident about the outcome of the book, but I believe that you do need to rethink parts of it.

The principal trouble is that I don't know what the book's about. You have introduced at least a dozen major characters, and at least half a dozen themes, and to do that in the first twelve thousand words or so seems to me likely to confuse your reader.

You may argue that you want all these characters and all these themes to play their part in the book and that the final result will be what reviewers used to call 'a rich tapestry'. But I'm not at all sure that that is the right way to write this kind of book. It is after all meant to be a commercial novel with a documentary background. It is not 'significant' and if it has a message at all, it puts it over almost unnoticed. It is a piece of entertainment—and I'm all in favour of entertainment! Now I think that this sort of book needs above all a strong narrative line, and a principal character, or perhaps pair of characters. I believe moreover that the reader needs to know from the very beginning what the theme of the book is and who the characters are that he is supposed to be interested in.

I feel it's rather like a symphony—the theme is stated first, and then comes the elaboration and the introduction of other less important strands. The symphony doesn't start with all the themes simultaneously and the variations and interweaving taking place before we have time to understand what we are about to hear.

Let's abandon that metaphor—I'm not enough of a musician to be sure of continuing it accurately—and get back to your book. As I see it (and if I'm wrong, then you will understand my point even more clearly) the main character is Walter, and the main theme is his position when he eventually discovers that his idol has feet of clay—will he decide that his loyalty is to his firm or to the man to whom he owes so much, and what effect will his decision have on the future of the firm, the other man and himself? Walter's complex marital situation, his involvement with the spare-time work, his discovery of his junior's treachery—these are all subplots, extremely important and relevant, but not the main thing that we are going to be told about.

Now look at the first dozen pages of typescript. Walter is certainly introduced early on, but he is always seen through another character's eyes, and the other character always seems to be the dominant partner. Can't we see Walter doing something, instead of letting him play the passive role all the time? In any case, however, I don't think that he should do too much in these early pages. At the moment you flash us through a whole series of little scenes, and I feel it would be better to build one of these up. Can you not invent some circumstance which will somehow reveal to us that Walter is an immensely loyal person—not a circumstance which is later to be used as part of the plot, but simply something which will, as it were, mirror the later situation? If you have Walter setting off for work in the morning, could you perhaps face him with the trivial little dilemma of where to buy his morning paper—from the man at the corner of his road, or from the man from whom he always bought it for the last fifteen years but whose pitch, since Walter has moved house, is a quarter of a mile away? I think the reader would immediately realise that loyalty is to be a main theme of the book. My actual suggestion is pretty feeble, and I'm sure you can think of something better, but the principle is right.

I believe it was Charles Morgan who applied the Biblical quotation about 'a little cloud... like a man's hand' to the business of play writing. He was talking of introducing early in a play an apparently insignificant reference to something which would become important later, using exactly the same principle as the clue which is planted early on in a detective novel and which later solves the whole mystery. Put in your little cloud at an early stage, your audience or reader will pick it up without difficulty (even if it is picked up subconsciously), and when you come to develop the theme later your audience or reader will feel in a receptive frame of mind for it, and will also feel a kind of satisfaction, because you've given the story form and a narrative progression.

I sometimes think that the classical dramatists had the right idea with the Unities—the Unity of Action, the Unity of Time and the Unity of Place. Perhaps the last of these is the least important, but there is certainly something to be said for having your story develop over a reasonably short period of time (though of course one can think of hundreds of successful books which sprawl over decade after decade!). But the Unity of Action—the idea of one main plot, and one only—is, I believe, very valid still, at least in the entertainment business.

One Unity that I am not very keen on is the Unity of One Character. I know that I said earlier that I wanted you to concentrate on one or two main characters, but if you do this please be careful that you don't put so much emphasis on your leading personae that all the people surrounding them are reduced to mere shadows or are totally cardboard. This is one of the reasons why first-person novels are so difficult, because very often the 'I' is the only fully realised character in the book. It works better if the 'I' is an observer, a narrator, rather than the main actor. But that is by the way.

Does any of this help? Whether it does or not, why don't you phone me or come and see me so that we can discuss it at greater length?

Above all, I beg you not to think that I hate everything in the book. Keep telling yourself that the book is going to be great and remember that I believe that too!

Yours,

44

Dear Gilbert,

Thank you for your letter. Of course I don't want to abandon the whole project! I have every confidence in you, and in the novel, and I am not saying that simply as a politeness. You must understand that, although I have made so many criticisms of the work you have done so far, they are of individual points and not of the book as a whole. It is rather as though I were going round my house saying that this room needs redecorating and I must get a new bath and re-tile the kitchen floor and paint the outside—all valid criticisms of the condition of the house, but none of them meaning that I am in any way dissatisfied with the house as a house. Do you see?

Please don't be discouraged. The writing of a novel of this scope is an extremely difficult undertaking and the number of authors who get it right first time is probably restricted to Tolstoy. (Did you know, by the way, that his work was regarded as a failure when it was first published?) Judging from similar big books that I have worked on it seems that even highly experienced writers like you do not find it easy to switch from the controlled and single-minded telling of a story like *A File of Poison* or *Condemned Sell* to the vastly different techniques of a long panoramic novel.

Believe me, I am not lying awake at nights wondering if you're going to get it right next time—I have no doubts at all. In fact I'm sure you're going to bring it off triumphantly. So cheer up and get cracking. I'm eagerly awaiting the next instalment.

Yours,

45

Dear Vic,

Thank you for your letter.

I am sorry that I didn't make myself clearer when I last wrote, and you're quite right to be irritated by a suggestion that you should cut your book without any guidance as to where the cuts should be made. I will go through the typescript again and make some specific suggestions on this point, but that will take a little while, and in the meantime I thought it might help if I put down a few guidelines.

First of all, repetition. I think if you check the typescript you will find a number of places where you have described the same thing more than once. I mean the same scene, the same physical characteristics, the same attitude of mind. We don't need to be reminded every time that the glen is beautiful, or that Doctor Macdonald is a crusty old man or that he limps or that he votes Tory. And you have two descriptions of a stag hunt. They're wonderfully well done, and I grant you that they are different—but to your reader onc stag hunt may well be pretty much like another, and I don't think he will want to go through the whole thing twice, or at least not in such detail. Why not give us the detail in the first one, and then cut the second so that we notice the differences, but aren't bored by going over the same ground twice?

Secondly, don't underestimate your reader. You really have no need to underline everything that happens. For instance, several times you have a dozen lines of dialogue, followed by a piece of prose in which you tell us how the characters felt as they were saying the words, and what their motives for saying them were. This is really quite unnecessary because if an author's dialogue is any good (and yours certainly is) the emotions of the characters are obvious from the words spoken and the reader is perfectly capable of working out for himself some of the subtleties that may lie behind them. You see, readers are well informed these days, and most of them know sufficient psychology to enable them, without detailed explanations, to understand the motives for your characters' behaviour and speech.

Thirdly, do make sure that your subplots have a real connection with the main story. For instance, the chapter in which you describe the upbringing of Hamish is very well done, but it really has no bearing on what is to come. Hamish is, after all, a comparatively minor character, and I believe that we could do without the whole chapter and that Hamish's actions would still be entirely acceptable and believable even if we don't know all the details about his early life. This is naturally the prime test: if you cut this word or sentence or paragraph or chapter, does the book really suffer?

Fourthly, have a look at the intrusive extra adjectives and adverbs. From time to time you seem to delight in a string of adjectives. As for the adverbs, this is particularly noticeable in some of the dialogue: *'Who the hell gave you the right to interfere?' shouted James angrily.* Angrily? How else could he shout it under those particular circumstances? You can cut 'angrily'.

Finally, have a look at the work of a writer like Graham Greene. Take a chapter of his and see how much you can prune from it. I doubt if you'll find very much that is spare. Then go back to your own book and try, as impartially as you can, to do the same kind of cutting.

I'll be writing again soon. Meanwhile, happy blue-pencilling!

Yours,

46

Dear Roger,

Thank you for your letter.

I am very happy that you have taken my criticisms in such a co-operative way, and of all the points that you cover in your letter there is only one that I am now in doubt about. This is the question of Miriam not recognising John when he comes back. I still can't accept it, even if it *is* based on a real-life situation. It's just another example of fact being stranger than fiction.

Let me tell you a favourite anecdote of mine.

As you know, I am involved in quite a lot of amateur dramatic work and this includes entering festivals at which professional adjudicators give their opinion of the plays we produce. One such adjudicator, the late John Bourne, told us that he was once commenting on a play in a festival and had occasion to remark that the two actresses playing mother and daughter in this particular piece worried him because they didn't look in the least like mother and daughter. Hearing some whispering and tittering among his audience he stopped, enquired what he had said to cause this reaction and discovered that the two actresses concerned were in fact mother and daughter in real life. He told the audience that he stuck by his opinion. He was not concerned with *real* truth, but with *dramatic* truth. Whatever the real-life relationship of the two women, if they did not look or behave like mother and daughter when on the stage in this particular play, then to some extent or other they had failed as actresses.

It is fictional truth as opposed to real-life truth that I am talking about now. Your real-life Miriam may indeed not have recognised her real-life John on his return, but when I read this situation in your novel I found it unacceptable. It just didn't ring true, within the framework of your story.

You may think this is unimportant. It is after all a comparatively minor matter in the novel. The trouble is that this kind of non-acceptance brings the reader up short, takes him out of the illusion that you have so carefully spun around him, makes him start questioning all kinds of other previously acceptable points in the story, and may make him stop reading altogether.

I do beg you to reconsider this point and alter that chapter accordingly.

If you cannot agree to do so, would you at least consider allowing one of the other characters to express, as it were on behalf of the reader, an incredulity about the matter? It is like coincidences—I think authors should avoid using them if they can, but if they can't help it, then the reader will accept the situation much more readily if the author, instead of just presenting him with it baldly, will say, 'By an almost unbelievable coincidence, such and such a thing happened...'

I shall look forward to hearing what you decide.

Yours,

47

Dear Eric,

Thanks for your letter. I'm sorry to hear that you feel you are not making progress with the new book. Believe me, the word 'stuck' sounds very familiar in my ears.

I can't think of any author with whom I've worked who hasn't suffered from this complaint at one time or another, and it's not something that you get only once like mumps or measles or pityriasis rosea (look that up in your medical dictionary! I only know it because I once had it!), it's a frequently recurring disease, and one that affects the most surprising people. I know one author who writes what might be called 'formula' books—the same basic plot, the same basic characters, the same basic background every time. How, one would think, can she ever get stuck? But she does. Regularly.

Another version of the disease is the feeling that the current book you are writing, and after some fifty pages or so have been completed, is banal, lifeless and totally unworthy of continuation. Again it happens to almost all the writers I know.

I tell you all this to reassure you that you are not unusual, and by implication to suggest that the disease is curable.

How does one cure it? Well, that's a little more difficult. One author I know, having sat for hours staring at the blank piece of paper in his typewriter, gets himself an enormous zonk of scotch, drinks it quickly and has another treble, and possibly a third. He finds that this unlocks the barrier and he can type happily for the rest of the evening. Next day he looks at what he has done in this semi-drunken haze, and—no, it isn't the best stuff he's ever written—it's usually a load of old codswallop and goes straight into the waste paper basket. But though he may have a hangover, he has also lost his hang-up.

That works for him. Whether it would for you, I don't know. And never let it be said that I drove one of my authors to drink!

Seriously, I have one piece of good advice to give, which has worked with many other authors who have found themselves in similar difficulties. It is to put the book away. Do your level best to forget all about it. Go and dig in the garden, or seduce your landlady's daughter, or take up butterfly collecting. Keep this diversionary occupation up for a minimum of a week. Then go back to the book and see if the block has disappeared. If it is still there, then try working on a new project for a while, or perhaps on a different part of the book—jump a few chapters if it is possible and you may find that you can cross the bridge backwards, if you see what I mean—or perhaps revise what you have done so far.

If this doesn't cure the trouble, then why not come and see me, and let's go through what you have done so far and see if I can disentangle it for you. But, Eric, that's a last resort—try to solve the problem for yourself if you possibly can. I'm sure if you do your best to forget about it for a short while, you will come back to it refreshed, and with all sorts of new ideas and enthusiasms—that'll be the work of the good old subconscious, which will have been slaving away all the time you are gardening or butterflying or dallying with the daughter.

Best of luck, and don't worry.

Yours ever,

48

Dear Ray,

Of course I will agree to the cancellation of the contract in view of what you say. I am sorry that you feel my comments are so unfair, and even sorrier that you don't wish to continue working with me. Perhaps you are right in suggesting that you are one of those authors who works best alone.

In case however you are tempted one day to set up a relationshp with another editor, may I beg you to remember that it must be, as they say about marriage, a give-and-take affair. If you will look through our correspondence about your novel-in-progress, I think you will have to agree that despite the fact that you begged for my help in the first place and protested your willingness to listen to me, you have in fact not accepted, even in the smallest degree, a single suggestion that I have made. Every point I have raised has been a matter for offended dignity on your part, or for bitter argument, or stubborn refusal to see any but your own point of view. You haven't either given or taken.

I'm afraid you'll think this letter even more unfair than my comments on your book. If so, try to forgive me. I genuinely wish you all the best and am only sorry that our great plan to be Thomas Wolfe and Maxwell Perkins didn't work out.

Yours ever,

49

Dear Molly,

Thanks for your letter. I am sorry to hear that you are finding it so difficult to begin the new novel, but I do understand how daunting all that research must seem.

I think there is a simple solution, which is to follow the advice of that very professional novelist, John Creasey, who said: 'Write now, research later'.

This obviously would not apply to all novels, and if you were going to write an historical which depended very much on the authenticity of its backgrounds and patterns of speech and behaviour, then you would probably be foolish not to do at least a large part of your research first. But even then you could do some of the writing at an early stage if you wanted to. After all, you don't have to research people, and people are the most important ingredient in any story. People are people the world over and throughout history (which, incidentally, always seems to me the outstanding quality of Shakespeare—that his characters are as valid for us today as they were when he first wrote about them). Create your people and fill in the details of their lives later.

Lots of authors that I know take far longer to prepare their background than actually to write their story. You have been lucky so far in that you have been able to write books with backgrounds and circumstances that are so well known to you that you can just write straight out of your head, as it were. Now that you have come up with this splendid idea for the next novel you are going to have to face sooner or later the drudgery of researching it.

Try doing it later, and let me know how you get on.

Yours,

50

To an author who asks for a firm rather than a tentative publication date for his book, and also enquires whether certain times of the year are better than others as publication dates

Dear Hilary,

Thank you for your letter. I'm not sure that I can answer as helpfully as I would like, but I'll try.

You see, a publisher decides on a given publication date with a number of factors in mind, but the factors themselves are so numerous and complex and the vagaries of book production such that he dare not make the date more than a tentative one in the initial stages.

Basically the publisher wants to publish the books he has signed up as soon as he can, so that he can begin to recoup the monies he has laid out on them, but he also has to consider his whole programme, the relationship of the particular book he is thinking about to the others on his list, the possible topicality of some of the books, the varying times needed for the production of different books, and other such matters. It would not do, for instance, to publish twenty-four books in February and none in March, nor does one want to publish all one's best books (or equally all one's weaker books) at the same time. I am sure you can appreciate too that a long, fully illustrated work, with an index and bibliography and complex acknowledgements, and perhaps diagrams and tables and so on, will often take much longer to go through the various processes than a short and totally uncomplicated novel.

Then of course, one's plans sometimes go awry. Perhaps the cover design for the book is very unsatisfactory and one decides to take the book out of schedule in order to produce a better design. This may mean also altering the publication dates of other books, for the sort of reasons given above. The same thing happens if a book is late in being delivered by the author. Sometimes, too, one comes up against the problem of the printer being unable to produce the book on time.

(This happens because, on the whole, printers are kept very busy—so much so that sometimes work has to be unavoidably delayed. Incidentally, when a book is a tremendous success and the publisher wants large quantities reprinted at very short notice and in a very short space of time, the printer's problems are intensified, and sometimes he has to displace one book from the schedule in order to make room for such reprints.)

I think that perhaps paperback publishers are more inclined to change their schedules than hardcover publishers. This is because hardcover publishers tend to produce finished copies of their books considerably in advance of publication date, and also because the paperback publishers work to a regular schedule of monthly publications, rather like a magazine publisher does. Paperback publishers also try, like jugglers, to keep a number of things in balance at the same time, which may not be of such importance to the hardcover house—a balance between the various categories (so that each month sees a reasonable quota of war books, romances, science fiction and so on), a balance between retail prices (so that each month has some comparatively cheap books and some comparatively expensive ones), a balance between the 'important' books in the month (i.e. those for which we have paid a lot of money and for which we expect major sales) and the less important, and finally a balance between the various months in the year. A delay over a cover design, a late delivery of a typescript, a sudden decision to add a book to the schedule because it is topical—anything like this can easily upset the delicate balance and cause books to be postponed or occasionally brought forward.

Now, as for the comparative values of different publication dates . . . Many years ago I began to write a book called *How to Write a Bestseller*. It was meant to be humorous and one of the chapters was concerned with publication dates and explained how your actual publisher can justify any month of the year as being a good month, or equally can condemn any month of the year if he wants to explain to you why your book has been moved out of it. For instance: 'January is a terrible month for publishers, because after the Christmas rush everything is dead in the bookshops'; or: 'January is a marvellous month for publishers, because all the shops have more room for books once Christmas cards and gift lines are out of the way, and everybody is busily spending their book tokens'. 'August is a marvellous month for publishers who use it, because the majority of them don't publish during the month and any books that do come out then are more likely to be noticed'; or: 'August is ghastly, because everyone is on holiday and the trade is at its slackest'.

In fact, publishers bring out books all through the year. Hardcover publishers still talk about their spring lists and their autumn lists, but this really refers more to the preparation of their twice yearly catalogues than to the notion that they only publish in the spring and the autumn. As for the paperback houses, their programme goes on fairly evenly throughout the year.

One thing is certainly true about publication dates—a really good book has rarely if ever been damaged by being published at the wrong time.

Again, I'm sorry I can't give you a definite date for your book. Once I feel more certain of it, I will let you know, but that will probably be much nearer publication.

Yours,

51

Dear Fred,

I'm sorry to hear that you are so disappointed about the publication date for your book. I should have warned you about the normal delay, and apologise for not having done so.

It really isn't because of slow working or inefficiency that it usually takes about nine months nowadays between acceptance of a book and publication (though there are lots of exceptions to this in both directions). Of course, the actual physical production of the printed and bound copies does not take this long, though even that is not an entirely speedy process. The big timing problem, however, comes about because it is no use simply producing copies of the book in time for publication if you have not prepared the way for publication by advance publicity and selling, and that in turn cannot be done without certain work having been carried out and material prepared even earlier.

It takes time to solicit orders from all over the world, and one cannot even begin to do so effectively until the booksellers and wholesalers can be shown material on which they can base their orders. In all this one goes through the usual routine. I know that there are those who say that 'because it has always been done that way' is the worst possible reason for continuing a given process, but the usual routine in bookselling is tried and tested and proved as the best way of selling books.

Let me list some of the things that have to happen to a book between acceptance of the typescript and publication. The book has to be designed (i.e. the format, the type size, layout of pages, and so on); it has to be copy-edited (punctuation checked, etc.); it has to be composed, or set in type; proofs have to be corrected; paper has to be ordered; a print quantity decided upon; the book has to be printed and folded and collated ready for the binder; the binding has to be designed and the necessary brasses (which will print the title and author's name on the binding) prepared; the binding cases have to be made; the book has to be bound; the jacket has to be designed; the blurb on the jacket has to be written; the blocks for the jacket design have to be made; paper for the jacket has to be ordered; the jackets have to be printed; the trade both in the home market and overseas have to be informed of the book and their orders for it obtained; publicity material has to be discussed, selected and prepared; the books (and publicity material) have to be despatched in advance so that they are in the shops ready for publication date. It really is quite a lot (and I have skipped several minor processes that also have to be gone through) to do in nine months, and bear in mind that I am talking about an ordinary, simple book, with no complications such as illustrations or index. Incidentally, the publisher pays for most of these processes before he gets any money back from the people to whom he sells the book—but that is by the way!

I mentioned earlier that some books take more or less time than others. Those that take more are usually held up at some stage or other—perhaps the author rewrites the whole thing at proof stage, or a libel problem arises, or some other matter which causes a delay. As for the ones that go through faster, well, yes, it is possible to publish a book in the course of a few days only, and it is sometimes done when the subject is desperately topical. It is achieved by cutting some of the normal processes, by allowing the book to take priority over all the other books the publisher is producing, often by paying the printer a premium to do the job quickly, and by everyone concerned making greater efforts than usual. One can't do it more than once in a blue moon. One can't very often speed up the normal nine months process to, say, seven months or six months, because whenever you do it you break the routine and frequently cause delays to other books in the list. I'm afraid this gestation period is nearly as inevitable as the human one.

One other important point that I forgot to mention earlier is that publishers have programmes. They try to publish their books at certain suitable times of the year and in batches of suitable numbers (obviously, one doesn't want to publish a hundred books in one month and ten in each of the other eleven months) and to some extent in a suitable balance of subjects and categories. Perhaps your novel or your biography or whatever could be ready in six months, but the list for six months from now might already have its full quota of novels, biographies or whatever. Moreover, one of the publisher's chief selling tools is his catalogue of forthcoming books, usually produced twice a year, and this public announcement of his wares forces him to decide on his programme at quite an early date.

Printers have programmes too, and to ask that a book shall jump the queue at the printer's can cause all kinds of disruption, making other books late. The printer works for a number of publishers, and has to try to keep them all happy.

I hope all this helps you to feel a little better about the delay. Believe me, most publishers would be delighted to get their books out more quickly—that would mean a quicker return on their money—but it just ain't possible.

Yours,

52

Dear Sidney,

I am not at all sure that I like the idea of your using a pseudonym for the new book. I agree that it is very different from anything that you have done before and in a much lighter vein, but I really don't think that it is likely to damage your reputation if it comes out under your own name. On the other hand I doubt very much whether I shall sell as many copies of it if I have to put it out as by 'Marmaduke Mugwump'.

Pseudonyms used to be very much the thing for a highly prolific author—hence all the names that John Creasey employed at various times in his career. But I am not at all certain that even someone writing as many books a year as he would need nowadays to disguise himself under a whole host of noms-de-plume. And if your output is not in the Creasey class then there is certainly something to be said for building your name up by letting it appear on all the books you write even if they are of differing types. You may get extra marks for versatility!

The only good reason I can see for the use of a pseudonym is if you're really ashamed of the book you have written and don't want the neighbours to know. In fact they usually find out, because it's very difficult to keep that sort of secret successfully.

Please be yourself—we love you as you are!

Yours,

53

To an author whose publisher has suggested changing the title of her book

Dear Claire,

Thank you for your letter. Of course I don't mind giving you some off-the-record advice.

I can understand that you're very upset at the idea of a title change, but I'm not surprised that it has been suggested. Not, I hasten to add, because I think your own title is such a ghastly one, but because I know that it is very easy for publishers to convince themselves that a title change is necessary. And I think it rarely occurs to them that this is a point about which the author may feel very strongly.

But what are the reasons for wanting a change? Well, the obvious one is that they may already have a very similar title on their list, or they may know that another publisher is about to bring out a book with exactly the same title. There is no copyright in titles, so one just has to try to avoid duplication.

Apart from that, I think the main motive for seeking a change is a belief that the existing title is unattractive, unmemorable, lacking in euphony, unsuitable for the book, or something like that. Everyone, from the office-boy to the managing director, becomes an expert in such matters—justifiably too, because, like so many things in publishing, it is a question of personal taste. Everyone is also aware of the vital importance of titles. Look at some of the great best-sellers of recent years and note how many of them have titles which (if you cast your mind back) were attractive and interesting and which stuck in your mind the very first time you heard them. All publishers, confronted by a title which seems to them undistinguished, will try to find one of those titles that have the air of potential best-sellerdom about them.

Of course there have been notable exceptions. The entire book trade tried to persuade Sir Stanley Unwin to change the title of *The Kon-Tiki Expedition* before it was published, partly because it sounded dull and old-fashioned and partly because nobody believed that the public would be able to remember the 'Kon-Tiki' part. The pundits were gloriously wrong.

I think really that my advice would be to phone your publisher and discover exactly why they want to make the change, how strongly they feel and whether they would accept an alternative to their own suggestions. If their objections are really strong, then I'd suggest you give in gracefully (though you could put up a fight about the alternative if you absolutely hate it and feel it misrepresents your book). On the other hand, if they seem uncertain, there's no reason why you shouldn't stick to your guns.

Let me know what happens.

Yours,

54

Dear Greg,

Many thanks for your letter about the illustrations for your book. There is no set rule about who should provide them. Publishers like their authors to give them the photographs, together with all the copyright clearances, and even a layout—they prefer this simply because it saves them work; but they are quite used to doing the job themselves. It does help though to have from the author a list of suggestions for possible illustrations.

Of course, in the case of drawings specially prepared for a book (as with an illustrated book for children), the publisher almost always takes the full responsibility for finding and commissioning an artist and approving his work, though again the author's ideas for subjects for illustration will be welcomed.

Hope this information helps.

Yours,

55

Dear Joshua,

I'm terribly sorry but I just cannot help you with an additional advance. The book hasn't yet got anywhere near earning the advance we paid originally, and that being so, our financial director wouldn't authorise an additional payment even if I were to ask for one.

I know that publishers used to be fairly free with money for their authors. It was all very nice for everybody—the publishers felt important and powerful, and that they were really being 'patrons of the Arts', and the authors didn't give a damn what it was doing for the publishers' psyches as long as they got the money. But in those days it was comparatively easy for the publisher himself to borrow money from the bank—nowadays it is difficult and very expensive.

I would help you if you came to me starving, or about to be shoved into clink for debts, or something like that—because that would be an emergency and in such conditions the firm can be as affected as I could be personally. But even then we'd need some sort of evidence of the situation and wc would be pretty cheeseparing in our handout. Publishers can't afford to be generous any more.

I'm really sorry.

Yours,

56

Dear Charles,

My secretary told me you had phoned—sorry I missed you—and she said that you sounded rather bothered. I can understand your feelings, but let me assure you that it is normal practice for a hardcover publisher to take a percentage of the monies coming from the paperback edition of a book. The amount involved ranges from 50% downwards, sometimes on a sliding scale according to the number of copies of the paperback which are sold, but is rarely less than 25%.

The reason why this huge slice is taken is not, as some authors seem to think, simply because Barabbas was a publisher. Very few of us are rogues and robbers. No, the argument goes like this: the hardcover publisher publishes your book; in doing so he ties up a very considerable amount of capital, and possibly spends a great deal of money in the actual business of selling the book; if the book is a success, the author and the publisher both benefit, but if it is a failure, the author at least has his advance (which may theoretically be returnable, but which in practice very rarely is), while the publisher may have lost a great deal of money—in other words, the publisher takes all the risk. But the principle involved is much more than that of just getting a return because he was willing to take a risk. He will also argue that if he had not published the book in the first place, then the paperback or broadcasting or anthology or whatever rights would not have been sold, because no one would ever have heard of the book. Moreover, he will tell you that he expends a considerable amount of time, money and experience in concluding the sale of these subsidiary rights. Therefore, in view not only of the fact that he has made the sale possible, but that he took a major risk in order to do so, he feels entitled to a share of the proceeds. I think it's a good argument.

I also believe that very few hardcover publishers would survive, at least in general publishing as opposed to educational or specialist publishing, if it weren't that they can depend on an income from subsidiary rights. A very high proportion of books is published initially at a loss, and on such books it is only from his share of other rights that the publisher makes a profit and manages to stay in business, ready to publish your next book.

It is because of this dependence on side income that hardcover publishers are increasingly in the habit of showing books to paperback publishers before they have bought them, hoping that the paperback man will say that he will buy the reprint rights, thus reducing the hardback man's risk, or sharing in it. In such cases it seems unfair that the maximum 50% should be exacted. Many hardcover publishers admit the justice of this argument and take a lesser sum, others are forced by agents to do so, but injustice still lingers around here and there. But then it does in all walks of life, and if you signed a contract giving your publisher 50% of the paperback money, I'm afraid you just have to accept it. Perhaps your surprise is due to your not having read your contract carefully enough. If you look at it, I am sure you will find that all the percentages that your publisher is entitled to take from subsidiary rights are listed there.

I can only suggest that you ask for better terms next time you sign a contract for a book. If you think it worth risking a move from your present publisher you might see if you can get on to the list of one of the hardcover houses which also has a paperback arm; if their paperback group also decides to take you on, you will probably receive the whole of the paperback royalty.

I hope this explains matters even if it doesn't make you feel much happier.

Yours,

57

To an author who asks about the publisher's progress in selling foreign rights in his book

Dear Bob,

Thanks for your letter. I'm afraid there is no good news to report yet. But don't assume because you have heard nothing that nothing is being done. Silence doesn't always indicate inactivity. When we publish a book in which we have control of the translation rights, we send copies to all our agents in Europe and they in turn start submitting the book to publishers in their countries, using of course their own knowledge of which publisher is likely to be interested. That is going on actively now with your book.

It can be a very slow business, but I hope before long we shall get a bite from a continental publisher. I must warn you however that it doesn't always happen, even with the most successful of books in this country. After all, when you think about it, it is reasonable that a book written by an Englishman and with an English background should not necessarily have any appeal to a Frenchman or a German. Anyway, we'll hope for the best.

I am sorry, incidentally, that I have not written to explain what was happening. One tends unfortunately not to give out information until it seems 'worth' giving out, and forgets that the poor author, in ignorance of the processes which in fact are ticking over nicely, thinks that nothing is being done and that we're a lazy lot of so-and-so's.

I'll write again as soon as there is anything to report.

Yours,

58

Dear Terence,

Many thanks for your letter. I am glad to hear of the German publisher's interest in your book and that you have sent him a copy, but I am not at all happy to learn that you have also given him an option on the German language rights.

I'm sorry to come the heavy publisher, but you really must not do this sort of thing. You have given us the right to deal with all such matters and the agents we employ to sell translation rights in our books are currently offering your book in a large number of continental countries, including of course Germany. The agents, highly experienced and very successful, work almost entirely on the basis of exclusive offers—in other words, any publisher to whom they offer the book in question knows that during the period that he is considering it he is the only publisher looking at it (a system which generally works much, much better—even if more slowly—than the auction method, when copies are sent out to several publishers simultaneously and offers are asked for by a given date). Your action in giving the book and an option to another publisher without the agent's knowledge could make all kinds of difficulties.

I know that you are rightly impatient for results, and that it appears as though we are doing nothing. I know too that you acted in good faith and will probably be flabbergasted to get this sharp rap over the knuckles. I am sorry if I have been too schoolmasterish in this letter, but the granting of an option is in itself a dangerous matter, because if you do not know the right technical jargon you could delay the selling of the rights or even allow the person to whom you gave the option the opportunity of buying the book for less than its market value. It really is a matter for experts.

I'm sure I can put it right, so don't worry about it—but please, please, don't do it again!

Yours,

59

Dear Colin,

I notice that you have quoted a large chunk of poetry in the middle of chapter 7 of your book, and I think I am right in recognising it as the work of a young man who published a first volume about a couple of years ago. His name escapes me. Have you cleared this use of his work with him and/or his publishers? You see, it is copyright material, and I believe wholeheartedly in respecting copyright.

After all, we earn our living from the printed word, and so (to some extent at least) does the young poet. Since he wrote the words why shouldn't he get first the credit and secondly a fee? The fee won't be very big, but it will make a small contribution to his income. If anybody ever wants to quote from your work I shall expect them to pay us for the privilege. And so will your heirs during the fifty years after your departure from this world during which copyright will still exist in your work.

If you want me to clear this matter up I will, but you'll have to remind me of the poet's name and, if possible, tell me who published him.

Yours,

60

To an author who asks about the design of book jackets

Dear Jennifer,

Many thanks for your letter with the suggestion about the jacket design for your book. I won't make any promises, but will discuss the idea with our Art Editor and see what he thinks.

Why do publishers so often put such awful jackets on their books? A good question. The brief answer is that they never mean to do so, but they are forever finding themselves at the mercy of their own meanness, or of their own blindness, or of the artists themselves, or of time.

Let's take those one by one.

Their own meanness. In fact publishers tend not to underestimate the importance of the jacket and many of them pay large sums of money to get a design that will be really attractive and which will also be commercial. Some do that. Others employ students or unsuccessful commercial artists and pay them minimal fees. Criminal! Or is it? Have those publishers discovered that in fact the cover design is not as important as everyone thinks, and that, at least in certain markets, it doesn't really matter very much what goes on the front of the book?

Their own blindness. A curious thing happens to publishers. Rarely will you hear them say before publication that this jacket is a bad one and that is a good one. No, all their jackets are good. And this is not just an indiscriminate turning of geese into swans—it is a genuine belief, based on the hours of work that have gone into the jackets, the publisher's past experience and the support of all his colleagues. This kind of confidence can be found even more often in a jacket design than in the book itself (and it is notorious that publishers, being optimists, believe blindly in the merits of all the books they publish). Anyway, it is only after publication that their critical faculties come into play. If the book is a success, they may then say, 'We would have sold even more with a better jacket!' and if it's a failure they may at last see the weakness of the jacket and put the blame largely on that.

The artists. Well, I don't want to upset all my artist friends, but I must tell you, in confidence, of my great discovery about artists. They can't read. I mean it. They just cannot read. You can give them instructions; you can say you want a painting of the heroine being kissed by the hero, that there is a description of the heroine on page so-and-so of the typescript and of the hero on page such-and-such, and that these descriptions reveal that she has short fair hair and blue eyes and he is very dark, with a beard. You are quite likely to get a Spanish-looking lady with long dark hair and a cleanshaven red-haired gentleman. Why? Because the artist was unable to read the passages concerned. The artist's own excuse is that 'it made a better picture that way.' Artists aren't concerned with being faithful to a story, they want to make a pretty design. Similarly, the lettering that goes on the jacket has to be most carefully checked, for an artist would never notice a spelling mistake—the word is a shape to him, not a word with meaning. Obviously I am exaggerating and you mustn't take me entirely seriously. But there is a glimmering of truth in what I have been saying. Of course there are many very competent and even brilliant commercial artists who will do exactly what is required. But frequently a publisher receives a poor design from an artist. Why does he accept it? Usually simply because there is no time to do another design, without upsetting his whole publishing programme for the book.

Time. Well, I've just mentioned this problem. Somehow jacket designs always seem to be late, however well one organises one's publishing business. And many, many of the poor jackets that you see around are there simply because there wasn't time to improve them.

Now why don't publishers give authors a chance to approve the jacket? I agree that it would prevent a lot of mistakes because the authors could point them out. Well, first of all, the publishers may not want mistakes pointed out, because it costs time and money to put them right, and the mistake that makes a tremendous difference to the author may mean virtually nothing in terms of sales—may even enhance them. The other problem is that authors may know how to write books and they almost certainly know the contents of their own books better than anyone else, but they don't necessarily know anything at all about how to sell them. The publisher does know how to sell books (or thinks he does) and he doesn't want anybody interfering with his jacket designs and possibly turning an inaccurate but commercial idea into a faithful but totally unsaleable one. Yet another problem is caused by the fact that authors are not usually practised at visualising a cover or jacket from a piece of artwork which is often very much larger than the jacket will be, which does not have the lettering on it, which has a large border of white around it—and you see, to show it at a later stage would make it impossible to change anyway.

Having said all that, you will be glad to know that there is an increasing willingness on the part of publishers to consult their authors about the jacket or cover design, and indeed on many other aspects of the publication, such as the wording of the blurb and publicity and promotion. However, I think most publishers would agree that while suggestions and comments from the author are welcome, and to be taken seriously, the final decision must be made within the publishing house.

Thanks again for your suggestions. I'll be in touch again when we have worked something out, and should be grateful at that stage for any further comments you may have.

Yours,

61

Dear Ralph,

I should be grateful if you would write me a little piece about your new book which we could use as the basis for the blurb which will appear on the jacket and in our catalogue.

This is a most important part of an author's job, and I sometimes wonder whether authors shouldn't be asked to provide it before they write the book rather than after. The point is that the blurb should give the raison d'etre of the book and also make it sound attractive.

I'm sure I need not tell you that the essence of this kind of writing is simplicity. The short, direct blurb is far more effective than the long, involved one. Apart from that I can only suggest that you should not be modest. If we think your claims as to literary merit, originality, brilliance and the rest are too fantastic, we can always cut you down a bit!

And that reminds me to ask you to note that I referred in the first paragraph of this letter to something which we could use 'as the basis for the blurb'. Don't be surprised if we alter what you write quite a bit. Like most publishers we see ourselves as something of experts in the writing of blurbs.

You will not be surprised to learn that I should have asked you for this a couple of weeks ago. So if you could let me have it by yesterday, I'd be most grateful.

Yours,

P.S. I look forward to reading it, and discovering whether you think of the book in the same way that I do. Once in a blue moon one finds from this kind of exercise that the author and the publisher have seen two totally differentthings in the same work. There's a chilling thought!

62

To an author who asks about our plans for the publicity and promotion of his book

Dear Kenneth,

Thank you for your letter.

Honestly, at this stage I do not know what we shall do in the way of publicity, but of course there are all sorts of possibilities.

Publicity and promotion breaks down into three main categories, depending on whether it is aimed at the trade, or at the public at large or at the potential buyer in your actual bookshop.

Most publishers spend a fair amount of time and money on publicising and promoting their books to the trade. They produce leaflets and order forms and brochures and all kinds of such material. They talk to the trade, they send them proof copies of the books, they may even send them little presents which have some connection with a particular book. They advertise in the trade press (i.e. *The Bookseller* and other magazines devoted almost entirely to books and bookselling, including some which are produced by various chain book stores). Much of the effort put into this kind of publicity and promotion seems to be worthwhile—though I suspect that the more gimmicky it is, the less effective!

Publicity and promotion to the public at large brings us first and foremost to the question of advertising in the national press. Almost all publishers would agree that this is a waste of time and achieves little in the way of selling, even if it flatters the author to see his book advertised. One must admit however that it has one very important side effect—without press advertising it is likely that most review pages in newspapers would disappear or at least be cut down, and that would be a pity, because reviews can help to sell books.

Reviews are a subject in themselves. Everybody in the book trade keeps asking when we are going once more to have a critic with the influence of Arnold Bennett, who, during the thirties, could make a book into a best-seller overnight simply by the power of his reviewing column. The problem is partly, I believe, that our critics today are less in touch with the man in the street than they were in the past—there are too many reviews of books that no one wants to read and which aren't really as important as they pretend to be, and too few of the popular books—but it is also due to the fact that we live in a different kind of world, in which hardcover books are not so readily bought as they were in the past, and in which cynicism has taught us not to revere the words of a single critic as undemandingly as our fathers did.

Nevertheless, reviews do sell books, and of course the publisher sends out copies to all the major papers and magazines, to any specialist organs that may have a particular interest in the book, to local papers in the neighbourhood of the author's home and to those radio and television programmes which review books.

Publicity and promotion to the public at large also includes such things as advertising on buses and in the London Underground (not very effective except as part of an enormous campaign, when all the components may have a cumulative effect), launching parties (going out of fashion these days, because journalists are no longer so ready to devote space to them), and radio and television interviews. The latter are extremely difficult to arrange. In the U.S.A. it is comparatively easy, because every city has its own television station, which occupies a fair part of its time on the air with interview programmes (they're cheap—you pay the resident interviewer, but the interviewees are only too pleased to come on for nothing or a nominal fee and tell you about their book or their invention or their heroism or whatever it may be, and you only need a couple of cameras and a simple studio), and the same applies with radio. In Britain, with its limited channels, it is far more difficult to persuade the programme planners to devote time to an author, unless he or she also happens to be a major celebrity. Even then, the competition to get on to the big interview programmes is intense and any author who makes it is lucky indeed. The value of such an interview can vary from nil to tremendous, depending entirely on what is said. I remember one of our authors being accused on television, quite unjustly, of having written a pornographic book. Next morning the sales rocketed!

Then there is the kind of publicity and promotion which takes place in bookshops. This is, in my opinion, the most valuable kind of all. I think that publishers spend too much time preaching to the unconverted (the public at large) and not enough time persuading the converted (those who regularly buy books) to buy more. The first agent in this kind of promotion is the book itself, its title, its author, its jacket (often incredibly bad), its binding and type. Of course not every house can have the elegance of Cape or (in the paperback field) Penguin, but some of us could perhaps try a little harder. Some of us may of course be more than a little anxious to cut costs and this is why, for instance, some paperbacks are printed in so small a type size that some readers find it very difficult to decipher.

Next there are posters, window streamers, displays, showcards and so on. And one can do considerable extra business in shops near to an author's home with special displays for a 'local author'. Signing sessions are somewhat unreliable—sometimes vastly successful, with hordes of fans and the author getting writer's cramp from signing his name, and sometimes disastrous, with the author and the publicity manager and the salesman and the manager of the shop making increasingly desperate small talk while all the customers stay away in droves.

As I say, I think the point-of-sale publicity and promotion is the most valuable, but it has to be realised that it is only available for a limited time. New books appear every day, and the bookseller cannot be expected to keep displays going for weeks on end unless the sales of the book in question are maintained at an extraordinarily high level.

There are a few other publicity and promotion matters one might mention, and particularly those which the author can be responsible for. Sometimes authors know reviewers or librarians or members of the public who might buy the book, and the publisher will always be glad to have a list of such people that he can circularise. I believe too that the more a writer appears in public the better, so I would advise authors always to accept invitations to talk about their work, to sit on quiz panels, or to serve on committees (providing of course that they can carry out these various functions with some degree of ability, though in most cases very little is in fact needed), because every person they meet may be a potential book buyer and may be persuaded by that meeting to go and buy that author's book, or at least to get it out of the library, which will perhaps add to your Public Lending Right earnings, and moreover the popularity of one book may mean that with the next book the librarian will buy more than one copy.

Now, how does all this affect you? The reason I cannot tell you yet is that we have not completed our scheduling for next year and therefore do not yet have a publicity and promotion plan fully worked out. I think you will probably be one of the lucky ones and get a fairly substantial sum of money and a considerable amount of time and energy devoted to your book, but just how it is spent will have to be worked out later. I say 'one of the lucky ones' because of course not all books get publicised and promoted. We publish up to thirty books a month and we just cannot push each one of them to the same extent. One book in the month will get a lot of attention, three or four will get some attention, and the rest will just be left to fight their own way on to the market—except that of course they will get space in catalogues and on order forms and time and trouble will have been spent on their cover designs and production and our salesmen will be doing their best to sell them. This sounds good but is obviously not as satisfactory as having an allocation from the publicity and promotion budget. Well, that's life. Some books get a lot, some a little and some only the minimum.

I'll let you know detailed plans—in particular anything that affects you personally—as soon as I can.

Yours,

63

Dear Mrs. Philpott,

I have just received your letter dated two weeks ago.

Yes, it would be a splendid idea to have illustrations in your little book on *Indo-Chinese Hors D'Oeuvres*, and especially a frontispiece in colour. An index would also be well worth having.

Unfortunately there are some difficulties in the way of including these extras.

Firstly, we have already sent the book to press (if you remember, I wrote to you last October saying that we were entirely satisfied, after the additional material which you wanted had been included, with the final version of the book, and that it would be going to the printers straight away). The printers have begun their work and if we were to start inserting illustrations at this stage they would probably have to stop all they have done, rearrange everything and begin again.

Secondly and most importantly, there is the question of cost. These little books are sold very cheaply, and the only way we can do this is by cutting all the costs that we possibly can. Illustrations are very expensive. First of all one has to pay the artist or the photographer; then one has to have blocks prepared, or film if a photographic method of printing is to be used; extra pages are needed in the book to accommodate the illustrations and extra pages mean extra printing charges as well as a greater paper usage.

All these problems are increased when it comes to colour work. Normally, to produce a colour frontispiece the paper on which it is printed would have to go through the printing machine four times. That costs money. And the preparatory processes are expensive too. And the photographer charges more for a colour print that for black and whites.

There is of course one good reason for including extra material, such as illustrations, and this is if one believes that extra sales will result from the inclusion. In your case I can't see a great sales inducement for adding them.

I am more unhappy about the index. It would certainly have been a good idea to have one, but again this would add extra cost, and I just can't see how it can be done. Had it been envisaged from the first, it might have been a different matter, but the length of the book is already pushing it near to the uneconomic end of the scale.

You see, publishers do try very hard to be businessmen. They publish books in order to make money. Now it is true that some of them are very much better at it than others. The ones who don't make money are the ones who don't keep a tight control on their costs. We make as much money as we can, and we do it by ensuring that we are selling our books at the right price as far as both the value to the customer and the profit to us and the bookshop are concerned.

I think it's an interesting point that when we cut a typescript we do so almost as often for financial reasons (to make the book shorter and so less expensive to produce) as to cut out unnecessary verbiage. Some authors have been very indignant about this, but usually it's much more difficult to convince the dull ones than the extravagant ones, if you see what I mean.

I am sorry to be so negative, and do hope you understand my reasons.

Yours sincerely,

64

Dear Perry,

Thanks for your letter with the most interesting idea for the odd-shaped book. I think it's most appropriate for the subject and would undoubtedly cause a great deal of interest. But, alas and alack, it's not going to be published by us, I'm afraid. Why not? Because odd shapes just aren't on. They're devilishly expensive to produce (because book printing and binding machines aren't made to cope with odd sizes) and when they get out into the market place, they often find it very difficult to get accepted because they don't fit on to normal shelves, and because (like publishers very often) booksellers tend to be conservative souls who believe that books should be in normal shapes and sizes, just as they believe in standard prices.

Pity. Actually, I think the idea is good enough to get by without the gimmickry of an odd shape, so why don't you let me have a more detailed synopsis and we'll see what we can do about commissioning the book.

Yours,

65

Dear Harry,

Many thanks for your letter.

Yes, it will be perfectly possible to insert a dedication at this stage, because fortunately the printers are still working on the proofs and have not actually begun machining (i.e. printing).

The one problem is that it will not be able to appear on a page by itself, but will have to be inserted above your list of acknowledgements. It can be done so that it will not look unsightly nor lack prominence.

The reason we can't give it a separate page is that to do so would mean adding at least four pages to the length of the book (the other three pages would be wasted of course) and also rearranging the printer's layout. It is a complicated business to explain, but perhaps you will begin to understand what I mean if you take a sheet of paper, fold it in half one way and then in half the other way; number the pages in the 'free' corner from 1 to 8, and then open up the sheet of paper and see where those page numbers appear. It will give you some idea of how the printer sets up various pages when he prints a book, and you will also see what the effect would be of suddenly inserting new pages in among the 'prelims' (the first pages of a book, including title page, biblio page, contents, etc.).

Incidentally, to take this a stage farther, pick out some books from your bookshelf and check up on how many pages they have, not forgetting to look at the prelims and find out whether they are included in the numbering of the pages of the book, and if not to add them in; add in too any blank pages or advertisement pages at the end of the book. You will find in the vast majority of cases that you end up with a number divisible by eight, or sixteen, or even more often by thirty-two. Printers use large machines which print several pages at once on one sheet of paper; the sheet is then folded and becomes a 'signature' consisting of four, eight, sixteen, thirty-two, sixty-four or even a hundred and twenty-eight pages, according to the size of the paper used and the number of pages it will accommodate.

I didn't really mean to give you this lecture, but it may be useful in the future so that you understand what can and can't be done at a late stage.

There is incidentally one other method of adding pages to a book—this is 'tipping in', when a single sheet (i.e. two pages) can be added. It is usually done at a late stage, often to correct some major error, and is extremely expensive, since it is done by hand.

Anyway, don't worry, your dedication will appear.

Yours,

66

Dear Mavis,

I am sending herewith the original typescript and two sets of proofs of your book.

You will see that one set of proofs has the words 'marked set' written on it. In it you will find marked any mistakes that the printer has spotted and also any queries that he has about perhaps a small error of fact or an inconsistency he has noticed or something like that. Will you please read this set, mark any other mistakes you may see, answer the printer's queries and make any alterations that you feel are necessary? You will see that marks made by the printer are in green ink. Please use red ink for correcting printer's errors and blue ink for alterations you wish to make (i.e. changes from the material as it appeared in the typescript).

There are some traditional signs and symbols that are used in the printing world to indicate various corrections that are to be made to type that has been set up. It is not necessary for you to use them, so long as you mark clearly what alterations should be made. On the other hand, if you can get hold of a list of the signs and symbols and use them correctly, the printer will be pleased, because then he will know exactly what you want. (A list can be found in *The Writer's and Artists' Year Book.*)

Now, a word about alterations. I hope you will not want to make too many. I know that it is very tempting for an author, seeing her work in print, to look at it with a critical eye and to want to change this word here and that phrase there and that paragraph there. But it all costs money—quite a lot of money. So please don't do it if you can avoid it.

If you must make alterations, there is something else to remember, and that is that the least amount of alteration the better. For instance, if you were to substitute in the middle of a paragraph the word 'tall' for the word 'high', comparatively little change would be necessary.

But if you substituted 'mountainous' for 'high', it might be necessary to carry a word over from the end of that line to the next line, and a word from the end of the next line to the one after, and so on to the end of the paragraph. Costly. Even more costly if the alteration is of much greater extent and means carrying lines from one page to the next to the end of the chapter. Even worse, if there is not enough room at the end of the chaper to accommodate the extra matter; then we are in real trouble, because we have to alter the pages through the rest of the book. The moral is that if you want to make alterations, try to see that your substitutions are the same length as whatever they are replacing; if you are inserting new material, see whether you can cut something already there to make room for the new stuff; use the space at the end of the chapter if you must, but only in the most desperate circumstances make changes that will lead to alteration of the paging.

I don't want to inhibit you totally from revising what you have done, but do be aware of the problems and reduce the re-setting of type as much as you can.

When you have finished marking your proof, would you please return it to me, together with the typescript? The second proof is for you to keep, and some authors like to mark the corrections in it and then make sure when the finished book appears that all the alterations were carried out. We ask you to return the typescript so that we and the printer can judge whether the corrections are due to errors by the printer or whether you have changed your mind since the typescript was completed and sent to press. In the former case, the printer pays the bill—in the latter case, we do (and if the cost of the changes exceed 10% of the cost of setting the whole book then you do!).

I'll look forward to having the proofs back as soon as you can manage them. By contract you have three weeks, but if you can do them earlier than that it will certainly help us.

Yours,

67

Dear Jim,

I do apologise for the fact that your punctuation has been altered and please do correct it back to the original version on the proofs. I am very sorry that you are going to have this extra chore.

May I explain how it comes about? You see, the majority of authors have very little idea of punctuation, and it is left to the publisher to put this right. In order to avoid having to mark up every typescript that needs this kind of attention, the publisher makes an arrangement with his printers to set down some rules about punctuation and other matters which will be applied to all the books he publishes. The rules cover such questions as whether to use single or double quotation marks, initial capital letters for the Deity, foreign accents, and so on.

Of course, there are occasions when the publisher marks the typescript with a request that the printer should follow it faithfully rather than using the 'House Style' (as these rules are called). That is what should have happened in your case, and I apologise for having forgotten to give that instruction. Naturally we will pay the cost of making the necessary alterations.

Do please forgive me. It is such a rare event to find an author who really knows his job that I should have been doubly aware of it all along.

Yours ever,

68

Dear Peter,

It is practically impossible to answer your question about how much money you can expect to earn from your second novel. From the first novel you must have already made about £20,000, with the hardcover sale, my absurdly large (!) paperback offer, and the American hardcover sale. This is pretty good going (indeed, it's miles above average), before the book has even been published, and especially as one can expect one or two translation sales, an American paperback offer, and possibly even a film deal. And of course there are other possibilities, such as book clubs and serialisations and radio readings and dramatisations and so on. But then it's a good book, and of course though it may be your first novel, you have undoubtedly been helped by having a known name. Believe me, beginners have a much tougher time.

But getting back to your point, we have to see what happens when the book is actually published. If it is a terrible flop (and it's possible, because it's so much a matter of luck in timing, in quality of reviews, etc.), you may find it hard to get anything like as much for the second book, and equally if it is a raving best-seller you'll be able to command a much higher price in future. What is more likely is that it will fall somewhere in between (that doesn't mean that I don't think the book has best-seller qualities—it has, but again I am trying to be realistic since so many books with great potential aren't lucky enough to make it). In that case, there is no reason to think that you will make less than £20,000 on the second novel, providing of course that you can maintain something like the same quality. (A little falling-off is allowed—indeed, it's almost obligatory for second novels—but you must demonstrate, as I am sure you can, that the first one wasn't just a fluke.)

The thing that worries me is that you seem to be asking this so that you can plan your life. If you are wondering whether you can give up your job and live in future on your writing alone, there's only one answer: for God's sake don't! It's such a chancy business that I wouldn't advise any author to go in for full-time writing until he finds that his part-time writing is bringing him in enough to live on and has been doing so for three or four years, or preferably longer. Then, perhaps, you can risk it. I am talking of course about authors without capital and without private incomes. If you have those, naturally it is a different matter. And if you made a great film sale of this first novel, you might be able to say: 'All right. I'll spread this $300,000 over the next four years while I'm building up my reputation.'

But one of the big problems is that you can so easily go wrong. The success of one book or a handful of books is not sufficient to guarantee even the acceptance let alone the best-sellerdom of the next book written by the author in question.

Let's talk about this again after the publication of the first novel. By then we may have a better idea of its potential, because foreign sales and perhaps a U.S. softcover deal may have come in. We may also have been given some signs about its reception here. If it becomes a big best-seller you may not only make a lot more money straight away from sales of the book and book clubs and so on, but you can possibly look forward to earning royalties for another ten, fifteen, twenty, fifty years.

Take that dreamy smile off your face, Peter, it may never happen, and probably won't. If it does, you can buy me a magnum.

Yours ever,

69

Dear Marion,

Delighted you can lunch with me on publication day so that we can really celebrate.

And yes, of course I shall be able to spare the time. It sounds to me as though you have the same sort of illusion that I had when I first started in publishing; I remember being terribly excited when the first publication date after I joined the firm came along. There was going to be a terrific hustle and bustle, I thought, with snarling men wearing green eyeshields, and boys rushing about with pieces of paper, while down in the basement the presses would be thundering away, and vans full of books would be leaving for all points south, north, east and west.

In fact of course none of this happened. My ideas had come entirely from Hollywood's version of the newspaper business. In a book publishing house publication day goes by almost totally unnoticed, and if anything it is quieter than usual.

You see, all the activity has taken place earlier—all the work of producing the book and selling it to the bookshops and invoicing and despatching the copies. All that happens on publication day is that the bookseller actually puts the book on sale (that is, if he's ordered any copies!).

Don't expect too much from your point of view either. I don't want to depress you, but I'd rather do so now than have you feel terribly let down on publication day and in the days just after. What I mean is—listen, the world doesn't change because it's publication day of your book. I think we shall do quite well with the book—we shall certainly try—and I think it has a great many of the qualities which are needed for success. But that success isn't going to come overnight. People aren't going to queue up to buy it, critics aren't going to review it immediately, the B.B.C. isn't going to ask to interview you. Success doesn't happen as suddenly as that.

Occasionally first books become best-sellers before they are even published. Why this happens I am never quite sure. There is a sort of unspoken conspiracy between author, agent, publisher, paperback publisher, foreign publishers and everyone else who is in on the act—a conspiracy which decrees that this particular book is one of the big ones. Sometimes it works, sometimes it doesn't— and one is never quite sure about that either. By the way, I should make it clear that there is always some justification for this decision that a book is going to be a best-seller—it can't happen with any old book—it has to have some element of specialness about it.

Best-sellerdom prior to publication also happens, not surprisingly, to established authors. But for others it's a long, hard grind. It does come once in a blue moon, unexpectedly and marvellously, to someone totally unknown, with a book that no one envisages as a popular success. If you should have such luck, let it be a wonderful bonus—but don't be disappointed if you join the thousands of other fine authors whose books do not sell in astronomic quantities.

I'll look forward to our lunch. It will be a pleasure to congratulate you again on one of the best novels I have read in a very long time, and to drink with you to the hope of its great and deserved success.

Yours,

70

Dear Michael,

I am delighted to be sending you your complimentary copies of *French Dressing*. I hope you like the look of it as much as we do.

May I give you a little warning, since this is your first book? Whenever a book is published, the author's friends and relations all seem to imagine that he has free copies by the lorry-load ready to distribute to anybody who wants one. All these people become predators, and how upset Aunt Mary can be if you give a copy to Cousin Philip but leave her out!

Now the advice I have to give is specific and firm. Make a list of the absolutely essential gifts—your Mother, the chap who gave you all that inside information about fashion shows, and so on. Keep two copies of the book for yourself—one to have in your bookshelf and one hidden somewhere in case the bookshelf one disappears (as it probably will). Even this brief list may involve you in buying more copies than the free ones you are entitled to. But stop there.

To all other enquiries reply with the information that your publishers are so mean that they have only given you six free copies, that you have had to give those to essential people, including some who helped you to write the book, and that your earnings from the book are so small that you can't afford to buy more copies. (They won't believe you, but stick to your guns!) Go on to tell them that the book can be ordered from any good bookshop, or in case of difficulty direct from the publisher. You may also say that your publisher has forbidden you to give out any more free copies, because he needs the sales.

Of course I am not being entirely serious, but you certainly need to be tough and ruthless with the inevitable cadgers.

All the best.

Yours,

71

Dear Bill,

Thanks for your letter.

Yes, I have read Jeremiah Clegbottom's *Sea Spray*, and I was impressed. I thought the characterisation was great, I really got caught up in the narrative drive, and I thought the actual writing was beautifully clean and often powerful. Bill, I think *Sea Spray* has a lot of qualities in common with your own novel, and if this is what you're really asking, I think you're as good a novelist as Clegbottom, and probably better.

But in the final analysis, as they say, that isn't what you're asking, is it? Your real question is simply why Jeremiah got such an enormous sum for the reprint rights in his book while I paid a mere £5,000 for yours. Right?

It's very hard to explain things like that to an author; in fact, it's quite impossible unless you are willing to accept one basic and incontrovertible truth: that we publishers are as emotional, eccentric, insane as any other group of human beings—or possibly, because of the unpredictable nature of our profession, we are even worse. Oh, we try desperately to be good businessmen, to weigh the pros and cons of all the business deals that come our way, but now and then we go off our heads and with a solo lunacy or sometimes with a kind of mass hysteria we offer and sometimes actually pay absurd sums for books that aren't worth it.

Let me take you in detail through the sort of thing that happens. I read a new book—*Sea Spray*, let us say—and I get very enthusiastic about it. I give it to someone else in the office to read, and he's wild about it too. So we start preparing estimates; we guess that we may be able to sell 100,000 copies at £2.95, and we work out the figures and discover that we could afford to offer something like £25,000 for the paperback rights.

Then we telephone the hardcover publisher. 'Fifteen,' we say,

'That's not nearly enough,' replies the hardcover man, and goes on to tell us that all the book clubs are after it, that the film has practically been sold, that a German publisher has paid a record sum for the book, and he expects to finalise deals this week in France, Italy and Sweden. 'Fifteen thousand,' he laughs contemptuously, 'you've got to be joking!' 'Twenty-five,' we say hastily. 'Still not enough,' he says. 'I've already got a higher offer from one of your competitors.' We say we'll think again and ring him back.

This is when we start getting excited. You see, the other deals that he mentions and especially the fact that one of our competitors has bid more than us all confirm our first judgment: this really must be a hot property. We revise our figures; by paring our profit, by thinking about a larger initial print figure and the possibility of reprints, we could double that £25,000. So we offer the publisher £50,000. He goes back to the other bidder, and back and forth and back and forth, and before we know where we are, the calculations are just telephone numbers, and we've persuaded ourselves that we could print a quarter of a million copies at a price of £3.95, and there we are making a big jump bid or perhaps asking the hardcover publisher what figure he'll settle for. He names a sum that almost takes our breath away, but we say 'O.K.' and the book is ours. And the next morning we start worrying about the wisdom of the deal.

You see? A sort of madness has taken hold of us and of our competitors, and the only winners are the hardcover publisher and Jeremiah Clegbottom. Or are they?

You would think that having been infected with this madness we would thereafter forever be on our guard against it, and that we, who pride ourselves on our commercial acumen and our strict control of costs and overheads and on our whole rational approach to publishing, would leave this sort of absurdity to our more emotional competitors. But there are two main reasons why we can't do so: the first is that, however hard we try, we remain irrational human beings, subject to pressures and enthusiasms and prejudices; and the second, terrible, frightening factor is that every now and then these wild extravagances are proved to be justified. When I was trying to buy the British reprint rights in *Lolita* by Vladimir Nabokov I telephoned George Weidenfeld and asked him what sum he would accept. The figure he named was £15,000, which may not sound very spectacular nowadays, but which in 1959 was the highest figure ever paid in Britain for reprint rights, and which, even for a book of such brilliance and notoriety, was at that time a mad, ridiculous sum to pay. Of course, we earned every penny of it and much more besides, and our profit on the book was enormous.

So perhaps you see why we allow ourselves every now and then to be caught up in one of these crazy ventures. Sometimes one wins an auction, sometimes it's the other firm. When you lose a book you can only hope that it's one of the unjustified sky-high bids, and console yourself with that well-known dictum in the trade that no publisher ever lost money on a book he didn't publish!

To get back to the point, why didn't this happen to you? Because we were astute enough to get in early and to make a bid of £5,000, which your publisher thought was a pretty good sum and which he accepted. Does that mean that he was a fool and should have waited to see if he could stir up a situation like the one for *Sea Spray*, with a mad auction, and all the paperback publishers bidding against each other? I don't know. Perhaps he was foolish. But he has to make a judgment. What happened with *Sea Spray*, by a previously unknown author, happens only once in a blue moon, and it is very difficult to recognise in advance which book it's going to happen with.

I'll give you another example. A hardcover publisher decided a few years ago that he had a really big book. It went to every paperback editor in London, and they all turned it down because the hardcover man wanted far too much money for it. In the end, I bought it, a long time after hardcover publication, for £2,000, which is probably what it is worth, but which is less than he might have got for it if in the first place he hadn't tried too hard to obtain an astronomic figure.

I seem to be rambling on and on. Am I proving anything to you? I hope at least that I'm explaining something, even if I'm not entirely sure what that something is.

All the explanations in the world don't alter the fact that you got only a tiny fraction of the amount that Jeremiah clawed in from the paperback rights in his book. No doubt you feel sore about it. I can't give you any comfort except to say that this publishing business, like showbiz, like professional sport, is partly a matter of luck. Jeremiah was luckier than you, and you've just got to accept that fact, my friend.

I believe that your book is better than Jeremiah Clegbottom's. What's more, I'm pretty certain that the £5,000 will be earned fairly quickly, and that we shall be paying royalties for quite a long time to come.

Think too of what will happen next time. Jeremiah and his publisher will expect to get at least the same amount for the reprint rights of his next novel, and they may well be terribly disappointed. Whereas you may be pleasurably surprised by the amount paid for your next book. You may be. Don't count on it. Read this letter again and realise with conviction what a mad, mad world publishing can be, and what a tremendous part chance plays in its successes and failures.

Forgive me for writing at such length, and let's wish ourselves the best of luck.

Yours ever,

72

Dear Leonard,

Many thanks for your letter.

I wish I could give you a formula for writing a best-seller. If I could I might give up publishing and write one myself! I don't think anyone can give you the answer—not even the authors who have written a best-seller, not even the publishers whose lists abound in them.

A best-seller is in fact very often totally unrecognisable as such until after it has been published. Many best-sellers have been turned down by a dozen or more publishers before being accepted. Others have become best-sellers at a very late stage in their lives—perhaps with the publication of a paperback edition, perhaps only when a film of the book comes out. Best-sellers are rarely created by publishers, though this sometimes happens when a firm, confronted with a book of outstanding ability, decides to promote it so heavily that they virtually force it into the best-seller class—but there are as many examples of this treatment failing as there are of its succeeding.

No, the creation of a best-seller seems to be almost entirely a matter of luck—the luck of getting the right kind of book at the right kind of time, with the right kind of title, and the right kind of author (a personable, promotable author, or a mysterious, recluse-type author can sometimes aid the process!), and the right publisher and the right reviews and the right timing of everything.

Some authors having achieved it with one book go on to write more best-sellers; others never manage to bring it off again. It depends whether or not the goddess of fortune continues to smile.

By the way, don't take any notice of best-seller lists that you see. Most of them are inaccurate—more in their omissions than in the titles included, and there are many best-sellers every year which never get mentioned.

Sorry I can't be more helpful, but I'll keep my fingers crossed for you (and for myself as your publisher!).

Yours,

73

Dear Stanley,

I am sending you a few fan letters which have arrived. I should perhaps explain that it is our habit when people write to us and ask for an author's address to reply that we are unable to supply it but if they wish to write to the author care of ourselves we will gladly forward the letter. The reason for this is of course that it protects you—it allows you not to answer a letter if you so wish without the danger that the person who wrote to you will arrive on your doorstep demanding to know why he hasn't had a reply. Equally of course he won't just arrive instead of writing the letter at all! I would suggest that you should take this a stage farther, and if you reply to any of your fans do not put your own address on the letter, but use ours as an accommodation address.

Yours,

74

Dear Celia,

Thank you for your letter. Yes, I too am very disappointed by the lack of reviews of your book. Why this should be I just do not know—it's simply another example of the way this whole business is ruled by luck. Copies of the book have of course been sent to all the major newspapers and journals, and in many cases they were accompanied by a personal letter to the Literary Editor concerned, pointing out that your book is one of which we think highly and which we believe has some importance. And nothing happens.

You say, 'I suppose this is better than bad reviews'. Well, not necessarily. The main value of reviews very often seems to be just that they mention the book, and whether they praise it or damn it doesn't always appear to have all that much effect on the sales. There are certainly a great many extremely popular and well-established authors whose books always seem to get torn to pieces (I'm sure you know the kind of review I mean—it comes usually at the end of the reviewer's column on new novels and it's terribly clever and frightfully witty and takes the micky on account of the book's length, weight and what the critic considers its insensitivity, vulgarity and so on), but their books still sell in vast quantities.

And then there are other best-selling authors who never get a review at all. It doesn't matter to them because their audience is already there, waiting eagerly for their next offering and no critic is going to make those readers stop being loyal to their favourite author.

In your case, it's a great pity that we have had this silence, because a comparatively unknown writer needs all the attention and mention he or she can get. I will contact one or two of my friends among the Literary Editors and see whether I can do anything. Don't bank on it, though, because I expect that they will say that they are sorry but they just cannot cope with all the books that are published every week, and yours is just one of the unlucky ones.

Keep your fingers crossed, and be comforted with the news that the sales so far aren't at all bad.

Yours,

75

Dear Melvin,

Your agent phoned to say that you were rather unhappy about *Time A'Flying*, or rather our attitude towards the book, so I am writing to explain matters.

It is quite true that we have sold out, and that we are not intending to reprint. The fact that your book is out of print must seem inexplicable to you, when it has quite clearly been a success.

In my firm we take a lot of trouble over deciding how many copies of a book to print. A great number of us is involved—those on the editorial side, those in the sales department, the publicity and art people, and, as a sort of referee and final arbiter, the managing director. Together we add up to a very substantial amount of experience. We take all kinds of things into account too: the editorial assessment of the book, the artwork on the cover, the book's history in its hardcover edition, the book's strength in relation to the other titles that we are publishing in the same month, the results that we have had with similar books in the past, our knowledge if any of what our competitors will be publishing in the same month, the author's reputation and, if he has written other books and particularly if we have published them, his past sales, the publicity and promotion plans, and anything else we can think of which may affect the book and its sales. Out of all this experience and with all these indications to help us we make a decision about how many copies of the book to print.

How often do you think we are right? I would say in no more than 10% of the cases. Mind you, we are not badly wrong in more than 10% of the cases either. But for the remaining 80% we either overprint or underprint slightly.

Of these two faults it would seem that the easier to correct is the underprinting. One can always reprint. But for economic reasons one cannot reprint just a few copies. A reprint has to be of a large number of copies, sometimes even as many as the original printing. Now if the demand is not sufficient to justify putting these additional copies into print, we are faced with the unhappy position that is currently affecting your book, *Time A'Flying*. Although we know we could sell a few hundred more copies, the re-orders are not coming into our office fast enough to make us believe that a reprint of several thousand copies would be justified.

If we had originally printed a slightly higher quantity, we would have been able to meet the demand in full. But if we had not been able to sell those extra copies it is quite possible, so finely balanced are a paperback publisher's costings, that we should have made a loss on the book. That's a situation we try desperately to avoid.

It is very frustrating for you. It probably won't be any consolation for you to hear that it is also very frustrating for us, but you may be better pleased to know that occasionally we re-issue after a period of some months books which, like yours, have sold out on publication and have not been reprinted. They sometimes find a new, larger market than they would have done if we had reprinted straight away. I can't promise that this will happen with *Time A'Flying*, but we can hope, can't we?

Yours,

76

Dear Frances,

I have now had an opportunity of checking with our Sales Department on the four shops you mentioned where your book was not to be found.

H. & B. Bloggs. Despite the assurance you received from the Manager we do not appear to have received any order from him for copies of your book. We checked with our representative, who told us that the Manager had refused to order it initially, despite the fact that he was informed that you live near his shop.

The Little Bookshop. I am not surprised that there are no copies of your book there, but it is not, as you were told, because we are inefficient, discourteous and care nothing for our authors. The Little Bookshop used to be an active account with us, but they have owed us approximately £300 since last Christmas, and since it is now September we have decided not to supply them with any more of our books until the debt is settled. Even then we shall want some assurance that they will pay up in future.

Henwood & Sons. Had you spoken to Mr. Henwood I am sure he would have told you that he had had supplies of the book, sold out and that he had re-ordered. The new supply reached the bookshop less than two hours after you were there. Unfortunately you were served by an assistant who obviously knew nothing and cared less.

Bath & Wells, Ltd. There were in fact twenty-four copies of your book sitting in a parcel in the store-room of this shop. The parcel had been there since the previous Tuesday.

If, my dear Frances, you detect some irritation in this letter you are correct in so doing and I can only hope you will forgive it. It does irritate me to find that someone like you is so ready to believe all the faults are ours. We are far from perfect, but we do actually make considerable efforts to sell our books. It doesn't do us any good to have them sitting in our warehouse.

Please note, out of your four bookshops one is doing a good job (though you happened to catch 'em on the hop), one is inefficient, one is dishonest, and the last won't order (and do remember that we can't force bookshops to buy our books or even to take them on sale or return).

A word of warning before I close this lecture. One author I know visits all his local bookshops regularly, and always makes clear his disappointment if he does not find his books on the shelves. One of the booksellers is a patient man and goes on ordering and selling the author's books. The other two are so fed up with his constant inspections and proddings that they refuse to stock his titles, and even the patient one has told us that it is no use our asking for a signing session next time we publish a new book by this author.

Cheer up. We've sold out of the first impression of your book and are reprinting, so it must be selling somewhere!

Yours,

77

Dear Carol,

I am very sorry to hear that you're so depressed. I suppose it is a condition that hits us all from time to time, but authors seem to be particularly prone to it. Perhaps that is because their job is really such a lonely one, and because it is impossible for most writers to judge accurately the quality of the work that they are producing.

I know of course that you feel you are getting nowhere and that you long for 'success'. It depends very much what you mean by 'success'. A great many authors—more perhaps than you realise—would be delighted to have published ten books, to have sold film rights on one of them, to have had each of them appear in a paperback edition and to have had occasional foreign sales. Moreover, many would envy you the knowledge that your publisher is always eager to have a new book from you and will send you a reasonable contract within a very short space of time after receiving the typescript.

On the other hand of course since your average income per book must be around the £2,000 mark, I can understand that you would look longingly at the authors who sell in vast quantities and make fortunes from their books. Why should they be so successful and not you? Well, some of the big names deserve every bit of their fame and their tax problems—for others it's a matter of luck. And what can you do about it? Nothing—except put every bit of skill and heart into every book you write (as I know you do) and hope that one day one of the books will click.

But Carol, don't get a fixation about it. Stop worrying, if you can, about other people's success, and think of your own. It may be much more modest, but it's still a success.

In any case, I am not sure that I don't prefer you as you are. So many of the really top authors—the ones who sell millions of copies and earn millions of pounds—despite having started off as nice, humble, ordinary people, have turned since their success into the most unpleasant, greedy, arrogant prima donnas. I would hate that to happen to you. But then of course you would be one of the exceptions, wouldn't you?—like Agatha Christie, whom I never met but who was, I am told, as unspoiled to the end as when she was first struggling to get a publisher to accept a book called *The Mysterious Affair at Styles*.

Cheer up! Come and have lunch next week and tell me all about the new book, and let us reassure each other about how nice and charming we'll remain when we're both millionaires!

Yours,

78

Dear Jocelyn,

Many thanks for your letter. The answer to your specific query will be available shortly. I am writing now because your request that when I give you the answer I should be completely honest is a remark which I must admit distresses me with its implication that publishers are ready liars. In fact I and most publishers that I know try very hard to be completely honest with our authors.

There are naturally circumstances in which one resorts to circumlocutions and white lies just as in ordinary life. For instance I will reject a beginner's hopeless effort with the information that 'our list is full'. If I am going to pass an author over to my assistant I will probably tell him that my work has been changed and that I have new responsibilities which make it impossible for me to continue to look after him—rather than saying outright that he is too unimportant for me to bother with any more. I am not perfect, and I will sometimes make excuses such as saying I have been rushed off my feet when the truth would be that I have been too lazy to deal with the matter or perhaps have forgotten all about it.

But I will never lie to an author if I can possibly help it about the important things. I will not tell him that we have sold more copies of his book than we have done (if only because the royalty statement will eventually expose my lie!), and if I hate his book or think it unsaleable I will say so as honestly as I can (if only because if I fail to do so I may find myself forced into publishing it), but I will always try to express my honesty in a way that will not hurt.

Anyway you can be sure that we shall deal with your question as honestly as we can possibly manage.

Yours,

79

Dear Jane,

Your letter gave me enormous pleasure. When an author's book is published it is right and proper that all the attention should be focussed upon her (especially when she is as easy to focus attention on as you), and that she should get all the praise and the congratulations.

But we publishers do put some effort into the book too, as you have kindly said, and it is a rare and delightful experience when an author acknowledges as you have so charmingly done in this letter that you feel a debt towards us—and when you include the whole staff rather than just the editorial people. In fact of course the debt and the pleasure are ours—but this does not diminish the happiness your thoughtful and friendly words have brought us.

Many, many thanks, congratulations, and may the book be as great a success as you and it deserve.

Yours,

80

Dear Theobald,

Yes, of course I would be willing to write to the Japanese Embassy and find out for you how many people currently belong to judo clubs in Nagasaki.

Yes, of course I will write to your American publisher to ask why you haven't received a royalty statement from him.

Yes, of course I shall be happy to book a room for you at the Savoy for a week starting tomorrow and get tickets for Thursday's first night for you.

Yes, of course I shall be delighted to order some books for you so that you can get the benefit of the trade terms which publishers allow each other.

Yes, of course you may come into my office at any time without an appointment and I will drop everything I am doing to listen to your account of your latest fictitious sexual conquest.

Yes, of course I will give you my home telephone number so that you can phone me on a Saturday evening and insist on talking about trivial matters for a full hour, despite the fact that I have told you that I have guests.

Yes, of course I will advance you £500 against your next royalties, though I know damned well they will show an enormous unearned balance.

Yes, of course we'll keep in touch after I retire—if you still want to do so when I am no longer of the slightest use to you.

Yours ever,

P.S. No, of course I'm not going to post this letter!

81

Dear Tom,

Thanks for your note and for all you say. Yes, I do love my job. I find it constantly exciting and stimulating. When I come into the office each morning I never know whether on my desk is going to be the most wonderful book I have ever read, or a writ for libel, or a complaining letter from an unhappy author, or a cheque for foreign royalties, or simply a dull old selection of routine letters.

And the books that I publish have the same sort of variety—somc of them I hate (for a publisher can't always publish just those books that suit his own personal taste), some of them I love, but they're all individuals.

Even more varied are the authors with whom I work—difficult or easy, endowed with genius or mere hacks, sincere friends or ready to be disloyal at the drop of another publisher's hat, conceited or modest, or any combination of all these and other qualities in any varying degrees you can think of. They are marvellous people to work with, and I try hard, as I believe every publisher tries, to help and serve them. It may not always seem that way, and it may even appear to the author that the publisher is working against him—but I beg you to believe that truly we are *on your side*.

Yours ever,

GLOSSARY

ADVANCE. The monies paid to an author in advance and on account of the earnings of his book. Often referred to in the U.S.A. as a 'guarantee'.

BACK LIST. After a book is first published it becomes, if it continues to sell, part of its publisher's back list. A publisher cannot exist on the sales of new books alone, but must have a strong back list of steady-selling titles. A new publisher's first concern must be to build himself a back list.

BERNE CONVENTION. An international copyright agreement. Countries which are signatories to the Berne Convention respect each other's copyright. The Berne Convention is still operative despite the Universal Copyright Convention, which, though effective, is not as universal as it was intended to be.

BIBLIO PAGE. The page of a book which contains the printer's imprint, the copyright notice, the printing history of the book, etc. It is usually on the back, or verso, of the title page. Sometimes also known as Imprint page.

BINDING. Hardcover books are usually bound by being sewn and cased, i.e. the signatures are sewn together and a stiff binding is then attached by means of the end papers. Paperbacks are more often 'perfect bound', i.e. the back edges of the signatures are trimmed, so that each page is separate, then glued and the stiff paper cover drawn on.

BLEEDING. Illustrations which go off the edge of the page (i.e. there is no surround to the illustration) are said to 'bleed'. A photograph used as an illustration in a book will frequently bleed on one or more sides.

BLOCKS. In letterpress printing illustrations and diagrams are usually printed from blocks. Line blocks are used where tones or shades of colours are not required. Half tone blocks are used for photographs and drawings which include, for instance, washes.

BLURB. The material about a book which the publisher prints in his catalogue and on the flap of his dust jacket. The blurb usually describes the content of the book in question and assesses its merits. Since the blurb is designed to sell the book it cannot always be relied upon to be entirely truthful.

BRASSES. The title and author's name on the binding of a hardcover book are not merely printed on but are 'blocked', and specially cut 'brasses', rather than type, are used for this purpose.

CASE. The binding of a hardcover book.

CAST OFF. A word-count usually prepared in a publisher's production department or by a printer and leading to an estimate of the number of printed pages that a typescript will make, given a specified type size and type area.

COLOPHON. A publisher's sign or trademark.

COMPOSITION. The setting up of type. Books are most often composed either by Monotype, a system in which each letter is cast separately when the compositor presses the appropriate key, or by Linotype, when the casting is not done until the compositor has completed each line.

COVER. See DUST JACKET.

CROWN. See PAPER SIZES.

DEMY. See PAPER SIZES.

DUST JACKET. The loose paper cover on a hardcover book, often carrying an illustration on the front and a blurb and the retail price on the front flap. Paperbacks do not normally have dust jackets, and their stiff paper bindings are called 'covers'.

EDITION. An edition of a book is not the same as an impression (q.v.). Each impression of a book contains the same material. Each edition is altered substantially from the previous edition.

END PAPERS. The four pages at the beginning and end of a hardcover book by means of which the case is attached.

FLATBED. See PRINTING PROCESSES.

FOLDED AND COLLATED. See SHEETS.

FOOLSCAP. See PAPER SIZES.

GALLEYS. See PROOFS.

GUARANTEE. See ADVANCE.

GRAVURE. See PRINTING PROCESSES.

HALF TITLE. A page of a book on which is printed the title of the book but not the author's name or that of the publisher. The first page of a book is usually a half title.

IMPOSITION. The arrangement of pages on a sheet of paper so that when the sheet is folded the pages will be in the right order and the type in the right position.

HALF TONES. See BLOCKS.

IMPRESSION. A printing of a book. New impressions of a book are reprints without changes having been made to the content. See also EDITION.

IMPRINT. The publisher's name printed at the foot of the title page is his 'imprint'. The printer's imprint, consisting of his name and address, is usually printed at the foot of the biblio or imprint page.

Imprint is also sometimes used to mean the publishing house itself—'That is a good imprint for an author.'

IN PRINT. Books which are 'in print' are available from the publisher, as opposed to those which have sold out and will not be reprinted and are designated 'out of print'.

But the phrase 'in print' is also used to indicate the number of copies printed of a book since it was first published—'I have fifty thousand copies in print of this book, made up of nine impressions,' or 'I have published ten of this author's books, totalling over two million copies of his works in print.'

JACKET. See DUST JACKET.

LETTERPRESS. See PRINTING PROCESSES.

LINE BLOCKS. See BLOCKS.

LIST. A publisher's list of titles—'We are glad to announce that X has joined our list,' or 'Our list contains science fiction and westerns.'

LITHO. See PRINTING PROCESSES.

OFFSET. See PRINTING PROCESSES.

OPEN MARKET. That part of the world which for English language editions of a book is not controlled exclusively by either the British or the U.S. publisher of the book. Broadly speaking, the Open Market usually comprises the whole world except the British Commonwealth (including ex-member nations) and the United States (and its dependencies).

PAGED GALLEYS. See PROOFS.

PAGE PROOFS. See PROOFS.

PAPER SIZES. Books are described by their physical shape according to the size of the paper used to print them and the number of pages that are printed on one side of the paper selected. For instance, a book designated as 'Crown 8vo (octavo)' will have untrimmed pages of 192 × 126 mm., since a Crown sheet measures 384 × 504 mm. and the '8vo' part means that eight pages are printed on a sheet. Similarly 'Crown 4to (quarto)' produces an untrimmed page of 252 × 192 mm. Other paper sizes used regularly include Demy, Royal and Foolscap.

PERFECT BOUND. See BINDING.

PHOTOLITHO. See PRINTING PROCESSES.

P.L.R. Public Lending Right. The Government-funded scheme which brings authors a token payment for the borrowings of their books from Public Libraries (provided that the titles are registered and the books achieve a minimum number of loans).

POINT SIZE. The size of type is measured in 'points' according to the height of the base of the type itself. One point equals 1/72". 12 points equal 1 em.

PRELIMS. The first or preliminary pages of a book, including title page, biblio page, contents, etc., before the text begins.

PRINTING PROCESSES. There are many printing processes used in the production of books. Letterpress printing is the kind practised by Caxton, involving the spreading of ink over type and the application of paper to the inked type. Other methods frequently used are photolitho ('offset' or 'litho') and rotogravure ('gravure'), both of which involve photography of printed pages or illustrations and the creation from the film of printing surfaces.

Some books (including most hardcover editions) are printed 'flatbed', the type remaining level and often stationary, and others (including most paperbacks) are printed 'rotary', when the type has been made into curved plates which are fitted on to a cylinder which prints the paper as it rotates.

PRINT RUN. The quantity of a book printed at any one time.

PROOFS. Proofs come in various forms. Galley proofs are long strips of paper on which long columns of print appear. This print has not yet been split up into pages, and galley proofs are used if large scale alterations or corrections are expected at this stage. Paged galleys are also long strips of paper, but the columns of type on them have been split into pages, though these have not yet been imposed. Page proofs normally look much like paperbacks. The type has been split into pages and the pages imposed.

RECTO. Open a book: the left-hand page is called the 'verso'; the right-hand page is called the 'recto'.

REMAINDERS. When a publisher finds that one of his books appears to have stopped selling, he may try to sell off his stock at very low prices to certain traders who specialise in such purchases. Books sold in this way are called 'remainders' and the people who buy them are 'remainder merchants'. The word 'remainder' is also a verb—'I shall have to remainder these books.'

ROTOGRAVURE. See PRINTING PROCESSES.

ROTARY. See PRINTING PROCESSES.

ROYAL. See PAPER SIZES.

S.B.N. S.B.N. stands for Standard Book Numbering (I.S.B.N. means International Standard Book Numbering), a system of coding books throughout the world so that each can be identified by a number.

SEWN AND CASED. See BINDING.

SHEETS. Before the printed sheets for a book are folded into signatures they are known simply as 'sheets'. British and American publishers sometimes sell each other sheets of a book, to save duplicating expensive printing processes. If the sheets have been folded into signatures and the signatures gathered together ready for binding into finished copies, these are known as 'folded and collated sheets'.

SIGNATURE. When a printed sheet of paper has been folded into pages it is called a 'signature'.

SUBSCRIPTION. When a publisher sells his books to booksellers and other trade outlets prior to publication he 'subscribes' them. Such advance sales are 'subscription' sales. The word 'subscription' is also used to mean the total number of copies of a book sold before publication—'This book has had a good subscription.'

SUBSIDIARY RIGHTS. All rights in a book other than those of the original publisher to produce his own editions of the book. Subsidiary rights include foreign, translation, book clubs, serial, film, radio, television, microfilm, anthology, digest, etc.

TITLE. Apart from the obvious meaning of the name of a book, the publishers use this word as a synonym for 'book'—'I am publishing twenty titles this Spring.'

TITLE PAGE. The title page of a book usually contains the title of the book, the name of the author (and the name of the illustrator, translator, or author of the foreword or introduction, or any other persons involved in the writing of the book, as apppropriate) and the publisher's imprint and colophon.

VERSO. See RECTO.

VOLUME RIGHTS. A publisher normally expects to purchase volume rights in a given book, i.e. the control of all forms of publication of the complete work within the territories granted to him in the agreement, whether or not he himself publishes them all. Thus volume rights include not only the original publisher's hardcover editions, but also book club, paperback, educational and other editions.

INDEX OF SUBJECT MATTER

(Figures refer to Letter numbers)